Dyslexia and Maths

Dyslexia and Maths

Julie Kay and
Dorian Yeo

Routledge
Taylor & Francis Group

LONDON AND NEW YORK

David Fulton Publishers Ltd
2 Park Square, Milton Park, Abingdon, Oxon, OX14 4RN

www.fultonpublishers.co.uk

David Fulton Publishers is a division of Granada Media Limited, part of the Granada Media group.

First published 2003

Transferred to Digital Printing 2009

British Library Cataloguing in Publication Data
A Catalogue record for this book is available from the British Library.

ISBN 1 85346 965 3

Typeset by Pracharak Technologies (P) Ltd, Madras, India

Contents

Foreword

This book is one of a series that provide practical insights for class teachers to ensure that it is possible for students with dyslexia to access different subjects in the curriculum.

In this book the authors, Julie Kay and Dorian Yeo, explain the nature of the difficulties that may be experienced by students with dyslexia in the area of mathematics. Although some of the difficulties experienced by students with dyslexia can be generalised to all subjects, in this book the authors specifically pinpoint particular difficulties that apply to mathematics. They discuss the language aspects of maths as well as the conceptual difficulties related to the abstract nature of the subject of maths. They, however, place considerable emphasis throughout the book on the strategies that class teachers can promote and students can use, all of which will help to ease the burden when tackling some of the difficulties associated with maths for students with dyslexia.

All the strategies suggested have been tried and tested by the authors; both are experienced practitioners and they are certainly writing from first-hand experience and this makes the book practical and invaluable to teachers of mathematics.

As well as containing a wealth of strategies for tackling many aspects within the subject of mathematics, the book also discusses the National Numeracy Strategy (NNS) and approaches relating to how maths is presented to the student, and also the important role of acknowledging learning styles.

We, as editors of this series of books, would like to congratulate Julie Kay and Dorian Yeo in writing an accessible, well-organised and structured book. We feel sure it will be widely sought by teachers of mathematics in secondary schools. We feel it will also be invaluable to primary class teachers who are seeking some further understanding of the difficulties that may be experienced by children with dyslexia in the area of number work and mathematics. This book therefore will be an essential source of reference and guidance in mathematics for all teachers.

Dr Lindsay Peer CBE, Deputy CEO and Education Director of the British Dyslexia Association
Dr Gavin Reid, Senior Lecturer, Moray House School of Education, University of Edinburgh

Authors' Biographies

Dorian Yeo was born and educated in South Africa. She lectured in English Literature at Natal University, South Africa. Shortly after coming to the UK she started teaching dyslexic children. In 1990 she became involved with Jane Emerson and Emerson House was founded in West London. Emerson House is a specialist centre offering intensive full-time and part-time tuition to primary school children with specific learning difficulties. Dorian teaches maths and runs the maths department at Emerson House, offers training for teachers and gives training days in schools. She has written a book, *Dyslexia, Dyspraxia and Mathematics*, which was published by Whurr Publishers in 2002. Dorian is interested in the broader area of children's cognition of numbers and has explored contemporary international research on how children learn about number.

Julie Kay has been a teacher of mathematics for twenty years. Starting as a primary school teacher gave her an excellent understanding of how to address the basic difficulties facing dyslexic students when learning maths. She has taught at Mark College, a specialist school in Somerset for secondary-aged students with dyslexia, since 1990, has been Head of Maths since 1994 and is now Head Teacher. Julie has co-written a series of worksheets designed for dyslexic students working on the NNS. She lectures on mathematics nationally and delivers in-service training for schools. She has conducted classroom studies with European partners into how dyslexic students learn mathematics and has co-presented the results at International and British Dyslexia Association conferences. Julie co-designed and delivered the first AMBDA (Maths) course, run in conjunction with Manchester Metropolitan University.

Chapter 1

Overview of Contemporary Mathematics Education in Schools

Background

Although some pupils thrive in just about any maths learning situation, it is a common observation that many pupils dislike maths at school and believe that they are bad at it. It is also often noted that adults frequently claim that they cannot do maths at all. Historically, school maths has certainly been widely perceived to be a difficult subject.

Throughout the last century, maths educationalists frequently expressed concern about the disappointing standards that the majority of pupils manage to attain in maths. In the past, government-backed reports into poor overall standards in maths often led to the introduction of maths teaching reforms. In England the most current of the many reform initiatives is the National Numeracy Strategy (NNS) (DfEE 1999), which will be discussed in some detail.

In the early discussions of dyslexia, it was often argued that dyslexic pupils do not experience out-of-the-ordinary problems in learning maths. In other words, in the early stages of thinking about dyslexia, it was not thought that dyslexic features might lead to difficulties in learning maths. It was felt that the learning difficulties which dyslexic children experience were mainly confined to language aspects of learning – and most particularly to difficulties with reading and spelling. Indeed it was sometimes suggested that dyslexic learners are usually good at maths. In the next chapter we will spell out in some detail the complex links between features which are strongly associated with dyslexia and which can lead to difficulties in learning maths.

In this chapter, however, we need first to explore the special nature of maths as a subject. We also need to outline some of the important changes that have taken place in maths teaching.

The special features of mathematics as a subject

What are the unique features of maths as a domain of knowledge, which have contributed to its widespread historical reputation as a difficult subject, and to its unpopularity amongst so many pupils?

There are a number of features of maths which distinguish it from most other subject areas with which children have to deal.

These features help explain why maths has always been hard for so many pupils, including dyslexic pupils, to learn. They also offer some insight, on the other hand, as to why some pupils find maths intrinsically easy to learn.

(1) In the main, maths is an abstract subject. Strictly speaking, the numeracy aspect of maths is based on concrete quantities (numbers of things in the world) and concrete relationships. However, maths as a domain of knowledge is usually presented to children in a very abstract way and this usually happens from very early on. Young children, and many older pupils, fail to make sense of some aspects of number work because they do not understand what they mean. Some pupils have a weakness in symbolic understanding and may have difficulty grasping the idea that *two*, *2* and *1 + 1* are the same thing.

On the other hand, some children seem to have an intrinsic (in-built, or early-developed) feel for quantities, which paves the way for a developing ability to visualise abstract numbers and abstract number relationships. This feel for numbers, or basic number-sense, seems to be closely allied with a degree of general visual-spatial competence.

(2)   Maths is a building-block subject. In essence this means that more advanced layers depend on knowledge of previous layers. This, in turn means that:

- Memory (long-term) and understanding necessarily play a key role in successful maths learning. In general, pupils remember most aspects of maths more easily if they have made genuine sense of them. It is very hard for pupils to remember aspects of maths that they have not understood. However, understanding does not guarantee long-term memory of what has been learned in maths. Pupils can also forget aspects of maths that they have successfully understood in the recent past and that they have managed to remember in the shorter term. In order to progress onto the harder, more demanding stages in the maths curriculum, pupils have to acquire long-term memory of, or have efficient access to, maths facts and they have to remember important concepts and procedures.

- If children fail to make progress at a particular stage in maths learning, they will tend to remain stuck at that particular stage. There are classic stages at which some children falter and become stuck, for example when multiplication and division is introduced, or when fraction and decimal work is introduced. A small but significant number of children become stuck at the very earliest stage of maths learning.

(3)   Calculation and problem solving in maths involve a thinking process, often with a series or sequence of steps. This in turn means that the working memory (short-term memory) aspect of global memory plays a key role in children's ability to make progress in maths. In fact, working memory plays a very important part in maths learning in two ways:

- At a more obvious level, the ability to make sense of a question, decide on a course of action, hold the question in mind, follow the steps through and keep on track until an answer is generated, requires a strong working memory. Research shows that the ability to visualise the maths question helps to support the working memory process to a very significant degree.

- Working memory also plays an important part in the process of learning many maths facts. Some facts, such as the times tables, are traditionally memorised as pure rote-learned verbal associations. Facts which are not required to be learnt as rote-learned verbal associations are learnt through repeated practice at working them out. Research has shown that knowing facts by heart through repeated practice requires an efficient use of working memory. It would seem that an efficient thinking process allows the learner to link the question or input (e.g. 4 + 5) with the outcome or output (in this case, equals 9). With practice at using efficient figuring-out processes, learners are able to remember (store in long-term memory) many of the frequently linked questions and outcomes as 'known' or 'in one' verbal associations.

(4) A greater emphasis is put on speed of working than in any other curriculum subject. This places a great burden on the pupil's working memory and on the long-term memory resources.

(5) Owing to the fact that maths is considered to be a difficult subject, many pupils have lower self-esteem in maths than in other subject areas. Low self-esteem tends to form a barrier to further learning. If pupils encounter real difficulties in maths learning this can confirm their feelings of inadequacy and may well lead to a self-fulfilling prophecy of failure.

A brief account of the most recent changes in maths teaching

Although ongoing concerns about maths education certainly meant that maths teaching changed in the course of the twentieth century, important continuities in teaching practices can also be traced. In other words, for a number of decades, many key features of maths education did not really change in fundamental ways. In the main, each new generation of parents found that the maths that their children had to learn was roughly similar to the maths that they had been taught when they were at school.

Insights
In more recent years profound changes have taken place at every level in the maths educational world. At the level of ideas, a number

of research-based schools of thinking about maths learning (which are scattered throughout the western world) have described in ever-increasing detail the developments which take place in the process of learning about number. This has allowed theorists and educationalists to gain better-informed insights into the ways that maths learning can be facilitated by teachers. Knowing more about how ordinary pupils learn number helps educationalists with the task of working out how the majority of pupils most successfully learn maths.

Recent comparative research has been concerned to investigate how children learn maths in other cultures and in alternative maths learning traditions. Significantly, some comparative research studies showed that pupils in the UK (and in the US) performed poorly in routine maths computation tasks compared with pupils from countries such as Japan, Korea and Hungary.

In some countries, such as the Netherlands, substantial changes in maths education became widespread from about two decades ago. A key, defining goal of the research-driven changes was to make all levels of number work as accessible as possible to the majority of pupils. Similar fundamental reforms have been implemented in South Africa and in many reformist maths projects and initiatives that have been set up in different parts of the world.

Curricular

Indeed these changes can be seen to be part of a general trend evident in the maths curricula in most countries of the westernised world. In England, the newer ideas about making maths teaching and learning accessible to greater numbers of children, and in this way improving overall maths standards, began to influence DfES thinking about desirable maths-teaching practices. This led to the decision to draft a new teaching policy and new teaching guidelines for pupils in the foundation maths years.

National Numeracy Strategy

Following a period of consultation and the evaluation of state-sponsored maths-teaching projects, the NNS was implemented in English state primary schools in September 1999. In order to try to raise standards, the NNS introduced changes of emphasis both with regards to *what* pupils should be taught in the numeracy part of maths lessons and *how* pupils should be taught number work. Since many of the changes are substantial and constitute quite a sharp break with past teaching practices, the NNS framework sets out the new teaching guidelines in a considerable amount of detail. A number of additional DfES publications have amplified the new teaching premises, principles and ideas.

Since September 1999, the majority of primary school pupils in England have learned maths in classroom practices that are based on the NNS. However, although all schools in the UK are required to follow National Curriculum guidelines, independent schools are not required to implement the changes introduced in the NNS. This has meant that numeracy is taught in a broad variety of ways in the private education sector. In a number of schools, maths continues to be taught in predominantly traditional ways. On the other hand, some independent schools have embraced the changes in teaching practices. Furthermore, newer maths schemes of work and materials are largely based on the NNS guidelines and framework. A number of independent schools have set out to try to incorporate the best of both worlds, introducing some reformist emphases, ideas and calculation methods, while retaining many of the traditional elements of maths teaching.

An overview of an institutionalised progressive maths teaching approach: The National Strategy

In order to understand changing ideas and policies in maths education more fully, it is helpful to set them in the context of more traditional approaches to maths teaching.

Traditionally, it is a central requirement that pupils become proficient at using the standard written methods of calculation; pupils are required to become more and more competent 'human calculators'. From this standpoint, maths is essentially about learning how to do harder and harder 'sums'.

As pupils have to learn the one right way of doing things for each kind of calculation, teachers inevitably dominate the teaching process. Pupils are relegated to a relatively passive role in the learning relationship; they are required to take note of what to do in each calculation situation and then copy, and above all remember, the right calculation procedure.

In traditional maths-teaching approaches, the multiplication facts are learned by rote and pupils are expected to internalise the addition and subtraction facts through large amounts of repeated practice at working them out. Pupils are not usually taught reasoning methods for working out maths facts.

In contrast to this, approaches such as the NNS set out to enable pupils to think more actively, logically and flexibly in all aspects of number work. A key goal of such approaches is to encourage pupils to be active in figuring out solutions to number problems. In the NNS approach, there is a much greater emphasis on fostering creative and independent reasoning. While pupils may need to be guided to become increasingly efficient thinkers, in the main pupils are also encouraged to use a range of different approaches to calculation. In line with this greater degree of freedom, pupils who are learning to think in new areas of maths are not required to employ the standard ways of recording their calculation steps. Instead, pupils learn the standard written methods of calculation after they have learned to use mental or reasoning-based methods of calculation. This is because the standard calculation methods are very abstract, condensed, difficult to understand, need to be written down and do not facilitate active thinking attitudes. The standard procedures are also generally unsuitable methods to use for genuine mental ('in the head') calculations. They therefore do not promote everyday-life numeracy.

Implications of the NNS for teaching

In order to be able to reason about number, pupils have to understand the ways in which numbers are made up of patterns and structures. Pupils need to spend time becoming familiar with a range of number patterns and with the base ten and place value number structures. They need to have a working understanding of abstract maths principles: for example, that addition and multiplication are commutative ($3 + 5 = 5 + 3$).

Independent thinking in mathematics also requires a sound understanding of mathematical concepts, such as the difficult concepts of multiplication and division.

In order to think creatively and flexibly, pupils need to develop good basic mental maths skills. In the NNS framework, pupils are ultimately expected to acquire by heart knowledge of maths facts, which then allows for very rapid recall of the facts.

Development of active thinking skills goes together with the development of an increasingly sophisticated grasp of the language of

cause an inability to calculate successfully in the longer term. Alternatively, teachers sometimes teach pupils one or two mental methods for each operation in a purely procedural way.

- The volume of work that pupils are required to cover, and the consequent pace at which pupils are required to work, means that many pupils fail to keep up and are left further and further behind.

In the next chapter we will see that some, and in many cases all, of these concerns affect the maths progress of a great many pupils with dyslexic difficulties.

Chapter 2

Issues for Students with Dyslexic Difficulties

In the introduction to Chapter 1, we noted that many early commentators did not see a connection between dyslexia and difficulties in learning maths. Research exploring the maths performance of dyslexic pupils throughout the last three decades and the work of educationalists who teach dyslexic pupils has shown that this limited view of dyslexia is incorrect.

In the gradually evolving literature on dyslexia and maths, there is broad agreement on the following aspects of the maths abilities and performance of dyslexic children:

- In maths learning, the spectrum of ability and performance of dyslexic pupils is very wide.
- Most dyslexic pupils experience a degree of difficulty with at least some aspects of maths learning, and usually with the acquisition of maths facts. Some dyslexic children learn to compensate for these difficulties in such a way that their ability to make progress is not impeded, and in some respects, where pupils devise or quickly learn to use effective reasoning strategies to figure out facts, may even be advanced.
- A small number of dyslexic pupils are conceptually able in mathematics. It is frequently acknowledged that some dyslexic pupils are gifted problem solvers. This means that conceptually able dyslexic pupils, who are able to compensate for their weakness in internalising maths facts, may be very good or even excellent at maths.

- A high proportion of dyslexic pupils experience substantial difficulties with many aspects of number work. Recently, a cross-cultural study found that 70 per cent of a sample of 10–13-year-old dyslexic pupils were performing at a level of more than a year below their chronological age (Chinn *et al.*, 2001) It is widely accepted that the proportion of dyslexic learners who struggle to make progress in maths is largely because many of the cognitive features that are associated with dyslexia make a number of key aspects of maths difficult.

- Among dyslexic maths learners, a number of studies show that two quite distinct maths learning styles, or characteristic ways of approaching maths questions, can be detected; these are frequently known as the grasshopper style and the inchworm style. Because the grasshopper-inchworm distinction has informed much of the discussion of the maths weaknesses and abilities of dyslexic pupils, it is important to explain the terms.

Grasshoppers are intuitive thinkers who are able to visualise questions. They tend to approach questions in a top-down or whole-to-part way. They generally have visual-spatial cognitive strengths. The thinking skills of grasshoppers are often undermined by weaknesses such as extreme impulsivity, dislike of step-by-step recording or jottings, poor maths facts knowledge and poor procedural knowledge. In other words, grasshoppers are often inventive, but cannot organise their thoughts on paper. As we will see, many grasshoppers find the standard ways of calculating difficult to understand. They frequently make the best progress in maths if they are taught mental ways of calculating and if they are encouraged to use those ways of calculating which they are able to visualise most easily.

Inchworm dyslexic learners do not have visual-spatial cognitive strengths. They are generally step-by-step thinkers who proceed in a bottom-up and linear fashion. They find it very difficult to form an overview of a problem. They do not easily picture problems as a whole. They try to remember the rules or recipes that apply in each area of maths. To work out solutions in most aspects of maths work they begin from what they understand to be the first step and then proceed by solving each next step until they reach an outcome.

The work of Steve Chinn, Julie Kay and Dorian Yeo has shown that many dyslexic pupils are inchworms and that there are smaller numbers of dyslexic grasshoppers. They have also found that younger dyslexic children are particularly inclined to be inchworms.

What are the cognitive features associated with dyslexia which can affect maths learning?

In essence, the key cognitive weaknesses which are part of the typical dyslexic profile and affect maths learning can be summarised in the following way.

The majority of dyslexic pupils experience:

(a) long-term weaknesses in memorising facts as verbal associations and in memorising step-by-step procedures
(b) working memory weaknesses
(c) sequencing difficulties
(memory weaknesses and sequencing difficulties lead to an over-reliance on counting)
(d) difficulties with many aspects of language.

In addition to these typical features, a number of dyslexic learners have:

(a) aural perceptual and/or aural memory weaknesses
(b) visual-spatial weaknesses and left–right orientation difficulties
(c) visual-perceptual difficulties and/or visual memory weaknesses.

Clearly the weaknesses outlined above are critical weaknesses in terms of the core demands of maths learning. As such there is a need to explore these weaknesses in detail. We note, however, that three important qualifications need to be highlighted:

- Many of the cognitive features that affect maths learning are actually interrelated and overlap in quite complex ways.
- Pupils learn maths over many years and some of the cognitive features assume a greater importance at certain times in the maths learning process than at others.
- Although dyslexic learners share many features, each individual pupil has a unique combination of strengths and weaknesses. These must all be taken into consideration if teaching is to be effective.

Long-term memory weaknesses in maths

Dyslexic pupils have considerable difficulty with the process of learning maths facts by heart. Many studies show that dyslexics have much poorer immediate recall of maths facts than their peers. This includes facts which are acquired through repeated 'figuring out' practice as well as facts which are learned as verbal associations. As we outline below, working memory difficulties contribute to poor knowledge of addition and subtraction facts. This is characteristic of younger dyslexic pupils. It is also well documented that dyslexic pupils have extreme difficulties acquiring facts as pure rote-learned verbal associations. Since the times tables facts are invariably learned this way, this considerably affects times tables acquisition. Many educationalists have noted that the majority of dyslexic pupils remember few tables facts as verbal associations. Indeed, following the work of Tim Miles, a very poor ability to quickly generate tables associations is often considered to be an indicator that a pupil might be dyslexic. Although poor maths facts knowledge may affect pupils at all stages of maths learning, it is a key part of number work at the primary school level.

Dyslexic pupils frequently have difficulty remembering calculation procedures in the long term, even when they appear to have mastered them. As was previously stated, working memory difficulties and sequencing weaknesses contribute in substantial ways to these difficulties.

Weak long-term memory resources partly explain why dyslexic pupils frequently fail to generalise knowledge. In any subject to be learned, automatised knowledge (knowledge which can be accessed from long-term memory and which does not require any thinking) allows pupils to pay attention to other aspects within that subject. Most pupils find it quite hard to generalise maths knowledge. As dyslexic pupils have relatively little truly automatised knowledge, they are particularly inclined to think along 'isolated tracks' in maths.

Working memory weaknesses in maths

Dyslexic pupils frequently have poor working memory capacity. This means that dyslexic pupils are able to hold less information and fewer steps in their working memory than ordinary children. In consequence dyslexic pupils may struggle to follow new calculation procedures. They often forget where they are in the reasoning process, forget what the next step is, and end up forgetting the question they were asked. Some dyslexic learners are slow to get the question onto the correct calculation path. Working memory difficulties can be particularly (and humiliatingly) evident in mental oral calculation work.

Poor sequencing skills contribute significantly to the working memory difficulties of dyslexic pupils. For instance, sequencing difficulties explain why dyslexic children frequently find it hard to remember counting sequences, count slowly, lose their place in counting processes, become stuck in counting tracks and have difficulties with all forms of counting backwards. Counting forms a vital foundation skill in many areas of maths. As outlined below, counting usually remains a skill upon which dyslexic learners depend. Poor counting skills add to the working memory burden of dyslexic pupils. Poor skills in counting backwards partly explain why dyslexic pupils find subtraction work very difficult.

Long-term memory difficulties contribute to working memory difficulties in maths. Firstly, poor long-term memory of maths facts means that dyslexic pupils inevitably face a very substantial additional working memory burden in many calculation situations. This is because they have to make a detour from the main calculation process to work out the unknown and needed fact, or facts. Secondly, difficulties in remembering calculation procedures can slow down the calculation process. Most frequently, difficulties recalling reasoning-based procedures mean that dyslexic pupils resort to basic and inefficient counting-based solutions.

As we have already noted, working memory weaknesses contribute in a very significant way to poor long-term knowledge of maths facts. This is because working memory plays a pivotal role in the process of acquiring by-heart knowledge of figured-out maths facts. Dyslexic pupils are frequently not able to link, in an efficient enough way, question and answer (or input and output) in their minds. Instead, the need to use a large amount of working memory means that the gap between question and answer is so large that it is not possible for the dyslexic pupil to make a binding link between the two. What generally happens is that the answer (or end-point of the reasoning process) is simply recorded or given by the dyslexic pupil, and giving an answer is often accompanied by a feeling of relief that the difficult process is over. This means that in future calculation situations the dyslexic pupil will have to work out the same facts all over again.

The link between memory difficulties and the counting habit

For dyslexic pupils there are three important repercussions of the working memory/long-term memory connection.

Firstly, as we have emphasised, dyslexic pupils frequently rely on various counting-based methods in calculation situations, and in particular in working out maths facts. Of course, younger primary school children are generally, and appropriately, expected to acquire the basic foundation addition and subtraction facts through using counting strategies. However, the working memory and sequencing weaknesses of dyslexic pupils mean that, unlike ordinary pupils, counting does not lead to by-heart knowledge of a growing number of facts. It also means that they generally become stuck with counting methods. Instead of acquiring the ability to recall increasing numbers of basic addition and subtraction facts, dyslexic pupils usually continue to count to work them out long after other pupils have ceased doing so.

Secondly, although most pupils are expected to learn harder times tables facts through purely rote means, many dyslexic learners rely on the strategy of step-counting the sequences of tables multiples. The laboriousness of long sequences of step-counting mean that here, too, dyslexic pupils become stuck with counting mechanisms and fail to internalise sufficient numbers of the tables facts.

Thirdly, in addition to using counting methods, most ordinary pupils begin to use logical reasoning-based methods for working out facts and are able to do so increasingly efficiently. Research shows that efficient strategy use requires small amounts of working memory and facilitates by-heart knowledge of facts. The majority of dyslexic children fail to devise reasoning methods and frequently have difficulty becoming confident and efficient strategy users. In a vicious-circle effect, using reasoning strategies in an unconfident and halting way requires precious working memory resources and fails to result in knowledge of facts. Most frequently, difficulties in the process of learning mental strategies for working out facts, mean that a large number of dyslexic pupils prefer to fall back on safe, but inefficient, counting methods. In summary, the majority of dyslexic pupils use counting to work out facts. Counting does not and cannot lead to knowledge of harder facts in the long term.

Sequencing difficulties

Key aspects of sequencing difficulties have been touched upon above. Sequencing difficulties also help explain why dyslexic learners struggle to remember sequences of instructions, and/or fail to remember the correct next step in calculation processes.

Difficulties processing sequential information affect the ability of many dyslexic pupils to see patterns in strings or sequences of numbers. This contributes to the difficulties which many dyslexic learners experience in trying to make sense of the structure of the base-ten number system. Many dyslexic pupils have difficulty generating base-ten counting patterns, particularly through base-ten collection points (for example, 80, 90, 100, 110 or 800, 900, 1000, 1100). Dyslexic learners also frequently struggle to manage counts away from specific values, such as 32, 42, 52, 62 and so on.

Poor sequencing skills also affect a rather different area of the maths curriculum and an important aspect of everyday life, the ability of dyslexic pupils to make sense of the complex sequences-within-sequences needed for the conventions of time. It is often observed that dyslexic learners have great difficulty learning to tell the time. It is also well documented that dyslexic pupils take much longer than their non-dyslexic peers to learn the order of the days of the week and the months of the year.

Difficulties with the language aspects of mathematics

The vast majority of dyslexic pupils have reading difficulties. Gaining access to the mathematics curriculum becomes more difficult as pupils progress through the education system because more emphasis is put on the language element once pupils move to secondary school. Pupils generally work more independently in maths as they get older. They have to be able to read a question before they can begin to understand what is required of them.

Mathematics has a language of its own and pupils have to learn the vocabulary of this new language. Terms such as *prime factor* and *denominator* are very specific to mathematics and pupils may not encounter them outside mathematics lessons. Terms such as *take away* or *difference* may be used in different ways in everyday conversations and in a mathematical context. Furthermore, many terms, such as the last two mentioned, refer to the same mathematical computation. This can confuse dyslexic pupils.

In mathematics, language is linked with symbols and a weakness in symbolic understanding is a well-documented feature of some dyslexic learners. Dyslexic pupils may have difficulties relating a specific kind of sum with spoken forms of the question. For example, they may not see that the number sentence, $5 \times 6 = 30$, derives from a problem such as 'There were 6 people on each table and there were 5 tables; how many people were there altogether?'

Aspects of our spoken number system confuse many dyslexic pupils. The spoken number twenty-one is not transparent but it is logical if you accept that 'ty' stands for ten. However, the 'teens' numbers, in the second decade, are inconsistent: if the 'teens' followed consistent rules, the number sixteen, for example, would be called 'onety-six'. It would be easier for dyslexic pupils to say numbers if all spoken numbers followed the same rules; 2636 could then be read as 'two thousand, six hundred, three tens and six'.

Language difficulties, linked with sequencing difficulties, make advanced multi-step problems extremely difficult for the student to access. Not only do pupils have to be able to read the question, understand the mathematical language and decide what calculations are appropriate, but they also have to be able to remember the order in which to carry out the operations.

Aural perceptual difficulties and aural memory difficulties

The many different counting sequences in maths are usually acquired as spoken sequences. Young dyslexic pupils with aural perceptual difficulties take longer with the first step of differentiating the words in spoken counting strings. This contributes to delays in learning to recite the counting strings. Together with general sequencing difficulties, aural discrimination difficulties also contribute to delays in noting patterns in sequences. This means that the sequences have, in large part, to be memorised. In learning about the number system, aural perceptual difficulties make it difficult to discriminate between the 'ty' and 'teen' cues for *ten*. This contributes to confusions which arise from the inconsistent structure of the spoken number system in the 'teens' decade. Similarly, dyslexic pupils with aural perceptual difficulties often have difficulty discriminating between six and sixth, ten and tenth, hundred and hundredth, and so on. This impacts on fraction work in maths.

A good memory for patterns of sound helps children remember complex sequences, such as the sequences of multiples making up times tables sequences. A good aural memory also alerts children to any mistaken steps that may be generated in sequence counting. Dyslexic pupils with aural memory difficulties do not remember sound associations. They are generally forced to rely on their weak addition skills to generate sequences, such as sequences of multiples, and have a poor ability to know that an incorrect step sounds wrong.

Visual, visual-spatial and left–right orientation difficulties

It is widely known that dyslexic learners often have strengths in the visual and in the visual-spatial areas of the brain. In terms of intelligence or cognitive profiling, dyslexic learners frequently have performance score strengths, in contrast to verbal score weaknesses. Similarly, but on a rather more informal level, it is noted that dyslexic children are often very good at 3-D pursuits, such as building with Lego, and that dyslexic adults are well represented in the architectural profession, among other creative careers. Visual and visual-spatial strengths are sometimes termed the 'compensatory gift' of dyslexia, or even, more simply, the gift of dyslexia.

In terms of dyslexia and maths, we have already noted that grasshopper dyslexic learners are good at visualising maths problems and that strong visualising skills can make dyslexic pupils good at the problem and puzzle solving aspects of maths. As we have also seen, visualising skills help support working memory processes, and may help to override some of the damaging consequences of sequencing difficulties.

It is important to understand that a number of dyslexics do not have visual or visual-spatial strengths. In fact a reasonably large proportion of dyslexic pupils have significant visual and/or visual-spatial weaknesses. In part this would seem to be because dyslexia frequently overlaps with another specific learning difficulty, *dyspraxia*. In essence, dyspraxia is a specific learning difficulty which involves coordination and left–right orientation difficulties. Dyspraxia is also highly correlated with visual and visual-spatial difficulties. Poor visualising skills in maths often means that pupils tend to process maths questions in inchworm-like ways. A very poor ability to visualise maths questions is strongly correlated with severe or profound maths learning difficulties.

Visual and visual-spatial difficulties frequently affect the maths learning ability of dyslexic pupils from the very earliest stages onwards. It is widely acknowledged that a basic feel for numbers, or number-sense, underpins a general competence in number work. Although maths is taught in a largely abstract way in most schools, number-sense is fostered through the very earliest experiences of working with, and taking in, concrete quantities. Visual-spatial difficulties generally affect hand–eye coordination and make it difficult for children to manage concrete materials effectively. Visual memory difficulties mean that children cannot draw on stored images of concrete work in order to make sense of subsequent number work.

Visual-spatial difficulties and/or left–right orientation difficulties frequently lead to directional difficulties in maths. Directional difficulties affect dyslexic pupils in two key ways. A commonly known dyslexic directional difficulty has to do with written number reversals. Primary school dyslexic pupils frequently write individual digits back-to-front and many dyslexic pupils have a tendency to reverse the order of two-digit numbers. Thus, for example, the number thirty-two may be written as 23. This is less common at secondary level.

Secondly, dyslexic pupils with directional difficulties usually have great difficulty remembering the correct ways to complete standard calculation procedures. The standard procedures for addition, subtraction and multiplication have to be executed from right to left, although numbers are written and read from left to right and basic number facts are also written from left to right.

Visual-perceptual difficulties and or visual memory weakness

Visual and visual-spatial difficulties affect the nature of the concept of number that children begin to develop early on. On the one hand, pupils with a feel for numbers generally begin to see patterns within numbers as well as connections between numbers. They begin to understand numbers as complex part-wholes. Understanding that numbers can be broken down in different ways is a key stepping stone towards being able to use mental reasoning methods in maths. On the other hand, children with poor visual-perceptual skills, a poor visual memory, and an associated poor number-sense, tend to see numbers in ones-based ways. This means they tend to see numbers as undifferentiated 'clumps' or 'lines' of ones. For instance, the number 12 is seen as all the numbers we need to count to reach 12, rather than as 'two more than ten' or 'six plus six'. One very significant repercussion of this is that pupils are inclined to see number operations (or sums) in ones-based ways. This in turn means that operations are usually understood as instructions to count all required solutions. In other words, poor visual skills and visual memory skills predispose children towards counting responses in calculation and make it difficult for them to visualise, and make sense of, logic-based calculation methods.

To summarise, a combination of many, or all, of the difficulties outlined above often works to compound the dyslexic pupil's belief that he or she cannot do mathematics. This, in turn, leads to a problem of low self-esteem. Research undertaken to analyse the error patterns in pupils' answers to questions has shown that dyslexic pupils are more likely to make no attempt than their non-dyslexic counterparts (Chinn 1995). This indicates that many dyslexic pupils would rather not attempt a question than risk getting it wrong.

Chapter 3

Dealing with Dyslexia in Mathematics Learning

General teaching principles

In broad terms, Chapter 2 established that if dyslexic pupils are to be helped to make the best possible progress in maths learning, they need informed teaching methods which set out to meet their complex memory difficulties. A linked consequence of the vulnerable memory resources of dyslexic pupils is that it is especially important that teachers ensure that their dyslexic learners genuinely understand all aspects of number work. In other words, the majority of dyslexic pupils require support in order to remember key aspects of maths at every stage of maths learning, and all of the aspects of maths which they are required to learn should be made as accessible or transparent as possible.

As we have suggested throughout, the sense-making and memory-support aspects of maths learning are interlinked in important ways. From a teaching point of view, however, it is helpful to cluster the teaching principles arising from these requirements under two headings.

Ensuring that dyslexic pupils understand number work

Using cognitive tools in appropriate ways

As we have seen, school maths is an abstract subject. It has been known for a long time that dyslexic pupils generally make considerably improved progress if concrete materials are used in carefully supervised ways to support all aspects of the learning process.

Concrete materials include:

(i)   Small *ones*, such as counters, coins, small plastic figures, individual sweets, etc. Because counters scatter easily and are difficult to pick up, rounded glass décor nuggets can be used instead. Dyslexic pupils may be distracted by a random mixed-colour selection of counters or nuggets. A single colour should be selected for many activities, but, in some situations, working with two colours can highlight a teaching point.

(ii)   Specially designed tools, such as base-ten materials (Dienes blocks) and Cuisenaire rods. An important advantage of base-ten materials is that the blocks are proportional. For example, a *hundred flat* is 100 times bigger than a *one*, or centimetre cube. Coloured Cuisenaire rods, too, are also one-centimetre-based, and are proportional. They represent the counting numbers to ten.

(iii)   Coins are real materials that pupils encounter in their everyday lives. Some pupils prefer working with coins than with artificial maths materials.

(iv)   Rulers are available in all classrooms. Metre rules are available in most classrooms. Rulers and metre rules can be used as ordinary number lines.

The NNS makes extensive use of rather abstract cognitive maths tools, such as number lines and hundred squares.

It should always be borne in mind that mathematical tools are intended to facilitate maths learning. Dyslexic pupils should only be encouraged to use maths learning tools in ways which genuinely support their understanding and which genuinely help develop their reasoning skills. This means that:

• Teachers should be clear about what aspect of maths learning the learning tool is designed to foster and precisely how the tool is intended to achieve this end.

• Teachers should ensure that pupils understand the way in which the tool is structured. For example, pupils must understand that a *hundred flat* is built of 10 *tens* and of 100 *ones*. To use three-dimensional base-ten materials effectively, pupils with spatial difficulties may need to be given time to explore the materials. This point applies to Cuisenaire rods, too. The interval-based structure of the number line, in which, for example, three is the interval, or jump between 0 and 3, is not understood by many pupils. Dyslexic pupils benefit from working with quantity-based number tracks, first. They also benefit from working with un-numbered 'emptier' number sticks and number lines, which are designed to represent the significant base-ten structures. Unsupervised use of ordinary number lines can encourage pupils to see larger numbers as a long line of ones.

- No maths learning tool should be used by a pupil as a crutch or as an answer-getting device. This is because the exercise of reading off answers from a tool is purely mechanical. It is therefore mentally passive, and facts and/or procedures are not learned, no matter how many times the reading off takes place. In particular, teachers need to take care that counters/glass nuggets are not used in entirely mechanical, one-number-after-another, counting-based ways. Number lines, too, are liable to be used by pupils in entirely mechanical ways. As soon as possible, pupils should be asked to have a go at figuring out solutions mentally; tools can be used to check the figured-out solutions.

- Teachers should not use materials to simply demonstrate concepts and procedures while the pupils passively watch; pupils learn most from cognitive tools when they are guided to use them in meaningful ways.

- Pupils should record concrete work or they should complete related mental or written activities immediately following concrete activities. Some concrete models can be built and then covered; pupils can refer to the models if they become stuck in the reasoning processes that the models are designed to make clear.

- At various points in the teaching process, teachers should evaluate whether a selected tool is facilitating the desired understanding. Understanding, and the difficult process of learning to reason, cannot occur when a pupil finds a tool difficult to make sense of, and/or when the pupil actively dislikes the tool. Teachers have to find ways to ensure that the tool, and the way it is used, is clearly understood (and better, is liked) by the individual pupil. If progress is not being made, the teacher should select a different tool, or teaching approach, to make the targeted aspect of maths clear. For example, teachers often use the numbered hundred square to help pupils understand important aspects of the number system. Many dyslexic pupils find it hard to make sense of the ways numbers are organised on the visually complex numbered hundred square, and they find the numbered hundred square tool difficult to visualise mentally. Where this is the case, teachers should use materials such as the structured number track, base-ten materials, or coins, instead.

Thinking hard about the language aspects of maths learning

A large part of understanding in number work is mediated through language. As we have seen, much of the language which is used in maths is in itself not easy to understand and dyslexic pupils frequently experience difficulties with the receptive (listening and processing) and with the expressive (talking) sides of the communication process. Careful consideration needs to be given to both of these sides of the language aspect of learning maths.

As far as possible, all teachers who work with dyslexic pupils should avoid lengthy explanations and lengthy sets of instructions for teaching pupils how to complete procedures. Instead, teachers should ensure that the necessary pre-skills for any new task are in place; maths language should be introduced alongside work with helpful maths tools and all tasks should be succinctly and clearly defined.

To ensure that the language used in lessons facilitates the understanding of dyslexic pupils, teachers should avoid introducing difficult terminology too early on in the learning process. Instead, teachers should start by using simple and easily visualised (transparent) maths vocabulary and should continue to do so for as long as necessary. Although dyslexic pupils eventually need to acquire the correct maths terminology, teachers who use terms before pupils are clear about what they mean delay understanding and learning from taking place. Once the conceptual understanding of pupils becomes secure teachers can successfully introduce increasingly sophisticated vocabulary. At first, difficult maths vocabulary can be used alongside the more colloquial and transparent words. Difficult mathematical terms should be regularly reviewed. To ensure that pupils rehearse maths vocabulary frequently, mathematical terms can be put onto simple rehearsal cards (see page 31).

Wherever possible, teachers should 'muse out loud' the kinds of reasoning processes pupils are presently internalising. It is important that pupils, too, are as actively involved as possible in the language learning process. For example, pupils can be asked to explain how they reasoned to complete a task. Where necessary, teachers can model or remind pupils of appropriate vocabulary. In situations where pupils fail to detect a mistake in the process of describing how they thought, they could be asked to physically demonstrate the reasoning steps, using an appropriate mathematical tool. In so doing, they should talk through the process once again.

In addition to these more general points about language, it should be noted that difficult-to-understand maths concepts make more sense to pupils if the concepts are situated in contexts with which pupils can readily identify. At present, many teachers equate the idea of putting sums into contexts with the rather specialised business of asking pupils to solve conventional written school word problems. As we will see, written word problems are highly condensed and stylised forms, and reading difficulties make them particularly difficult for dyslexic pupils to make sense of. It is highly recommended that teachers use informal and meaningful spoken situations, which are worded in everyday language, to help make maths accessible. Genuinely engaging spoken situations can be woven into lessons in a natural way rather than treating them as a specially allocated block of work. Concrete maths materials may sometimes be used as additional support. Introducing real-life situations in this way has the additional advantage of helping dyslexic pupils prepare for dealing with written word problems.

Supporting the memory difficulties of dyslexic pupils

Structuring teaching carefully

We have suggested that it is particularly difficult for dyslexic learners to remember arbitrary sequences of steps in maths, or, in other words, to acquire procedures parrot-fashion. Understanding why the steps in a maths procedure are necessary helps to support working memory processes. It is precisely because dyslexia is associated with memory difficulties in maths learning, that it is all the more essential that dyslexic pupils are helped to reason in maths. However, the ability to reason in maths also entails memory costs, particularly when dyslexic pupils do not have compensatory visualising abilities. As we have indicated, foundation understanding and many skills have to be in place for pupils to be able to reason in maths. This means that maths teaching needs to be very carefully structured.

Most importantly, this means that:

- Teaching has to build on previously acquired understanding and skills. This means that teaching has to start from the dyslexic pupil's current level of knowledge. To know where to begin, it is usually useful to give dyslexic pupils a diagnostic assessment (see page 86).
- Teaching steps should be sequenced in terms of difficulty. When new areas are being explored, or difficult areas reviewed, teachers should micro-adjust the level of difficulty of the maths problems which pupils are asked to solve. Within an individual learning session, problems should be increased in difficulty until pupils are appropriately challenged. In the longer term, teachers should carefully select the appropriate next step in the teaching programme. Some dyslexic pupils can only make progress if their learning programme is structured in very small steps; others make large leaps in learning in those areas of maths they have a feel for.
- All tasks should have a very clear immediate purpose and equally clear longer-term goals. If the teachers of dyslexic pupils cannot clearly identify the maths learning value of a task in textbooks or maths schemes it is generally best if the task is omitted.

Teaching maths facts especially carefully

Particular care has to be taken with the crucial but complex process of helping dyslexic pupils learn maths facts. As we have seen, all the evidence suggests that dyslexic pupils cannot learn facts in purely rote ways. We have also seen that dyslexic learners tend to rely on counting strategies in figuring out maths facts but we have emphasised that engaging in longer sequences of counting does not lead to by-heart knowledge of maths facts.

In other words, both rote learning and counting are ineffective learning routes for dyslexic learners. If teaching is to be effective, helping pupils master reasoning strategies is a key part of helping dyslexic pupils learn the maths facts. It is crucial for teachers to understand that:

- Dyslexic pupils need to be taught ways of reasoning (fact-derived strategies) to work out all maths facts.
- Most dyslexic pupils need to be given structured help with the process of learning to reason increasingly efficiently. It is important to help dyslexic pupils achieve efficiency in maths fact

derivation for two key reasons. Firstly, practice at using efficient reasoning processes helps most dyslexic pupils begin the process of automatising maths facts. Secondly, efficient reasoning allows speedier access to maths facts and supports the smoother functioning of working memory in calculation situations.

Three vital further points need to be made:

• Although learning to use reasoning strategies substantially reduces the long-term memory burden of pupils, they have to have a foundation of memorised facts to use as a starting point from which to reason. It is important that teachers identify and target a small set of essential facts that pupils need to know in each area of maths. These facts, the key facts, are the indispensable blocks for reasoning that need to be earmarked for particular over-learning and review purposes. (Key facts can be put on rehearsal cards so that they can be practised until they are known by heart, see page 31).

• Working memory weaknesses frequently impact on the actual process of learning to derive facts through reasoning. We have noted that dyslexic pupils are often:

(a) slow to process maths facts questions
(b) slow to determine on a course of action
(c) slow to execute reasoning steps.

One very significant teaching repercussion of working memory difficulties is that although some visually able grasshopper dyslexic pupils learn fact-derived reasoning strategies relatively effortlessly many pupils are not able to do so. Indeed, many dyslexic pupils feel overburdened and become confused if they are required to practise a number of different ways to figure out facts.

This means that many pupils with maths difficulties do best if the structured teaching approach adopted in the early calculation stages helps them to learn one easy-to-follow universal fact-derived strategy for each of the four operations. As the understanding and the confidence of less able dyslexic pupils grow, they are generally able to modify the basic strategies which they have learned or even devise new strategies for themselves. They often do so in increasingly self-assured ways.

• Working memory difficulties also mean that dyslexic pupils frequently need more time to complete the process of figuring out facts than most ordinary pupils. Two repercussions flow from this:

(a) In order to begin making progress in learning maths, many dyslexic learners simply require that teachers make the necessary allowances to give them sufficient thinking time in maths facts work.

(b) It is also true that, if dyslexic pupils are going to become more efficient thinkers and speed up their ability to access facts, they require to be given considerable amounts of practice at using the reasoning processes. This means that teachers need to build sufficient over-learning practice into all aspects of maths facts work.

It is, nevertheless, important to remember that while sufficient practice allows the majority of dyslexic pupils to access maths facts in increasingly efficient ways, there are a number of dyslexic pupils whose working memory functioning is so weak that they are simply not able to reason particularly quickly. Teachers need to realise further, that this slower pace of reasoning inevitably has important repercussions on the general speed of work of these pupils.

Times tables

With regards to dyslexic pupils, it needs to be clearly understood that all of the general points made above also apply to the process of acquiring the **times tables** facts. We have touched on the fact that the tables are the special case body of facts which are very widely taught and learned as pure verbal associations.

Very briefly, the tables facts are usually taught through rote verbal association methods because the times tables are objectively difficult for all pupils to learn. This is largely because there are so many different *times tables* sequences or tracks of multiples to master. The connections between individual multiplication facts are also complex and appropriate connections between facts are difficult to discern. For instance, the connections which allow for generalisations in learning tables facts, are much harder to see than they are in learning addition facts.

To make it possible for pupils to learn tables facts as verbal associations, the many tables sequences from which the facts come are usually turned into forms of chants, poems or songs. Each individual tables fact is embedded as a line in a long sequence of lines. The words of each line have to be remembered exactly. To recall a tables fact learned this way requires that pupils recall and generate, absolutely exactly, the appropriate line from the entire, long sequence. For example, the question 'six times seven is . . . ?' has to be completed by retrieving from verbal memory the exact verbal association 'forty-two'. No thinking is involved in this process. The process is entirely reliant on the premise that pupils have a strong memory for verbal associations.

However, while most ordinary non-dyslexic pupils have reasonable or even good verbal memory resources, it is a feature of the cognitive functioning of the majority of dyslexic pupils that they have a remarkably poor ability to remember maths facts in the form of verbal associations. Most dyslexic learners simply cannot remember the exact words making up individual tables lines. In other words, no matter how many times a line such as 'six times seven equals forty-two' is rehearsed, it is very unlikely that such a dyslexic pupil will be able to recall that 'six times seven is' is associated with 'forty-two'.

To sum up it needs to be accepted by teachers that it is simply not productive or appropriate for dyslexic learners to be required to learn the times tables facts using the traditional rote-learning methods. It should be made clear, too, that while a number of dyslexic learners may have some success at remembering tables facts as pure verbal associations in the shorter term, the associations are soon forgotten. Over many decades, research has shown that rote times tables learning is a very unsuccessful longer-term learning route for dyslexic learners.

Teaching advanced calculation skills carefully

The question of how to help dyslexic pupils learn more advanced calculation procedures for each of the four operations in maths is a multi-faceted one and needs to be given careful consideration.

First of all, teachers need to make decisions about which procedures would seem to be most appropriate to teach to specific dyslexic pupils. The age of the pupils, the nature and the severity of their particular difficulties, and the pragmatic question of how they have been taught at school all need to be taken into consideration.

We have noted that the standard column-based procedures are particularly abstract, condensed and difficult to understand. This means that most pupils are forced to execute them in purely memorised, recipe-like ways.

We have also noted that mental calculation procedures are generally easier to understand than the more traditional procedures. Working memory difficulties and problems remembering seemingly arbitrary sequences of steps certainly make the standard methods particularly hard for most dyslexic pupils to remember. Conversely, some of the easier-to-understand mental calculation procedures are relatively easy for dyslexic pupils to learn and may therefore be considered much more dyslexia-friendly than the standard procedures.

Ideally then, the majority of dyslexic pupils should spend time learning accessible mental calculation methods, in the first instance, and should make the transition to learning to use the standard procedures in carefully structured ways.

Ideally, too, those dyslexic pupils who have difficulties which make the standard column procedures extremely difficult to remember, should be allowed to continue using mental methods for as long as necessary. However, many dyslexic pupils with poor visualising skills and poor 'thinking' abilities, who have to use the standard written calculation methods in class, are not easily able to generalise the understandings gained from mental calculation work to formal work in columns. These pupils generally do not 'switch' well from one approach to another. It is often advisable to help dyslexic pupils who are in these situations learn the standard calculation procedures from the outset.

Questions also arise in relation to mental procedures. The written standard procedures have to be executed in one prescribed way. In contrast, just as there are a number of different kinds of fact-derived strategies for figuring out facts so too there are a number of different ways to reason to work out larger calculations.

Some grasshopper dyslexic pupils are able to learn a range of different mental methods and thrive on their freedom from the hard-to-visualise standard methods. On the other hand, many less visually able dyslexic pupils become confused if they are required to learn a number of different ways to proceed. Some mental methods of calculating are also more difficult to understand than others and are therefore more difficult to learn and remember.

The parallels with learning fact-derived strategies are clear: dyslexic pupils who have difficulty remembering procedures make best progress if they are taught one universal mental method for each operation.

Rehearsal cards: a practical, time-effective way to support long-term memory difficulties in maths

Rehearsal cards are a set of cards, unique to each individual pupil. They are intended for pupils who have marked memory difficulties in maths. They contain maths information which pupils have been taught in a multi-sensory way but which they find difficult to remember. Each individual pupil is given a small set of cards to practise under supervision of an adult. Sets of rehearsal cards should include about 5–25 cards, depending on the age/ability of the pupil. Once the pupil has automatised the information on a card, it can be removed. The cards should be rehearsed as frequently as possible, and preferably every day. Teachers should monitor the pupil's knowledge of their set of rehearsal cards as frequently as possible. Some suggested uses for rehearsal cards include:

(a)   *Vocabulary cards:* these cards target any aspect of maths language which a pupil has difficulty remembering. The problem word is written on one side of the card and a pupil-friendly, transparent definition is written on the back. For example, Question: What does *multiply* mean? Answer: Multiply means '*groups of*' or '*times*' *or* '×'.

(b)   *Key Facts cards:* these cards can be designed to target the essential facts. For example, Question: What are the key facts in the 4 times tables? Answer: $5 \times 4 = 20$ and $10 \times 4 = 40$.

(c)   *Facts cards:* Ordinary facts cards target what the pupil presently finds difficult to figure out. The to-be-practised fact or question is written on one side of the card. Both an appropriate figuring out route and answer are written on the other side of the card. For example, Question: What is 6×4? Answer: $5 \times 4 = 20$, so $6 \times 4 = 24$.

Effective teaching suggestions

Teaching the number system

The number system is complex. There are differences between how we say numbers and how we write numbers. There are also important structuring features that the spoken number system and the written number system have in common. It is important to ensure that dyslexic pupils have a sound understanding of both aspects of the number system.

(1)   Counting activities help pupils understand the overall base ten structure of the number system and familiarise pupils with the conventions of the spoken number system.

(2)   Building numbers helps pupils understand the structure of written numbers.

Counting

As we have suggested, dyslexic pupils who are not good at numbers usually have a ones-based concept of numbers. In terms of the number system, this means that dyslexic pupils see big numbers as long lines or bigger clumps of ones. A key job of teachers is to enable pupils to see individual numbers in relation to the structures. For instance, the number 19 is certainly 19 ones, but it is also 1 away from 20 and 19 is also 9 more than 10.

Concrete counting activities

Dyslexic learners often have difficulty counting objects. Frequent miscounting affects basic number-sense. Counting difficulties often lead to errors in counted outcomes in the earliest calculation situations and may contribute to a dyslexic pupil's dislike of numbers. From the beginning, many pupils need instructions on how to count objects in an organised way. Dyslexic learners should count objects frequently, move objects as they count and count rhythmically to synchronise the counting words with the counted objects. They should also pause to take in the quantity that has been counted.

The number line form is a very adaptable tool and can be made accessible to dyslexic pupils from the earliest learning stages onwards. It can be a very useful device for foregrounding the base ten structures and for locating numbers in relation to structures. However, as we noted, it is helpful to prepare for number line work by working with number tracks, number sticks, and un-numbered number lines.

The decade structure to 100

(1)   Dyslexic pupils learn a great deal from counting quantities of ones into a track formation. The quantities can be estimated first. Pupils count the ones into structured lines of tens.

ooooooooo   oooo = 14

ooooooooo   ooooooooo   ooooooooo   oo = 32

(2)   Pupils are asked to find individual numbers on a simple tens-structured track or on a structured bead string.

(a) ooooooooo   ooooooooo   ooooooooo   ooooooooo

(b) ooooooooo   •••••••••   ooooooooo   •••••••••

'As quickly as you can – without counting from the beginning – show me the numbers 30, 40, 10, 1, 21, 9, 39, 22 . . .'

Teachers should draw attention to the differences between the 'teen' numbers and the 'ty' (or decade) numbers. They should say these word endings in an exaggerated way.

(3) Pupils should work with emptier structured number tracks and structured number lines. For example, pupils can be asked to build tracks of selected numbers, using base-ten materials, for example 31 can be built from a train of three tens and one one. This can be contrasted with 13.

(4) ○○○○○○○○○○●●●●●●●●●● can be represented in structured number line form as

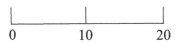

0   10   20

on a structured number line.

(5) In concrete number track and structured number line work, pupils can be asked rounding-based questions, for example which tens number is 38 closest to? . . . and 22? . . .

Counting large quantities concretely

It makes a big difference to dyslexic pupils if they practise counting the different higher value sequences (that is, in tens, hundreds and thousands) using base-ten materials. It is important to practise counting through the base-ten collection points, for example 90, 100, 110; 900, 1000, 1100. Counting should target the difficult transitions through collection points, for example pupils can be asked to start counting materials in hundreds from 800. It is important that pupils grasp the way in which smaller units of value build up to make larger units of value and vice versa. In cross-counting activities, quick counting in hundreds (500, 600, 700) can give way to much slower counting in tens (710, 720, 730, . . . 780, 790, 800) and then the pupil can return to quicker counting in hundreds again.

Oral counting

Counting needs to be as automatic as possible. When dyslexic pupils have acquired a feel for the larger value counts, they should practise oral counts.

For example, dyslexic pupils can be asked to:

(a) count from different starting points, targeting base-ten collection points

(b)   practise broken chain counting

(c)   count backwards, short ways, to cater for sequencing difficulties, for example 420, 410, 400, 390, 380

(d)   practise cross-counting in different values

(e)   practise large value counts, such as counting in tens of thousands and hundreds of thousands; target collection points and practise cross-counting

Coins can be used in place of base-ten materials to aid the transition to complex forms of counting. Coins help some dyslexic pupils to count in tens away from rounded values. Pupils start with a given value and add 10p each time, for example 12, 22, 32, 42. This shows, in a concrete way, that the units digit remains the same when each ten is added.

Counting: fractions and decimals

Counting activities help to put fractions and decimals into the context of ordinary whole numbers.

(a)   Real or pretend sandwiches/mini-pizzas/small cakes can be cut into halves, thirds or quarters, and then counted. The pupils build and articulate the wholes along the way: one-third, two-thirds, (three-thirds) one, one and one-third, one and two-thirds, two . . . This can be followed by oral counting exercises, for example 'Count in quarters, please, starting from the number 4. Count backwards in fifths, starting from the number 3'.

(b)   Primary school dyslexic pupils can cut a number of French sticks into tenths and count them using the decimal conventions. Structured metre sticks or rulers can be used for counting decimal parts-to-wholes in the same way: 'zero point one, point two, point three, . . . point nine, one, one point one, one point two, . . .'. Once again concrete counting exercises can be followed by oral counting activities: 'Count in tenths starting from thirteen point nine' 'Count in hundredths, starting from two point eight five'.

Written counting based activities

Exercises which involve completing given sequences can be designed on the same principles as the activities described above.

Learning to make sense of the written number system

In the spoken number system, the units of the different values are all given names. For example, we say, four thousand, six hundred; four thousand, seven hundred etc. In the written number system, the value of the units making up larger numbers is determined by their position or place relative to each other. This is why the written number system is called a place value system. In written numbers, the place of the digit alone tells us its value. This means that the written number system is very abstract and condensed, and many aspects, such as the crucial role zero plays in holding the place of values, are difficult to grasp.

To make sense of the place value conventions, dyslexic pupils should engage in different kinds of number-building activities:

(i)   Pupils should have the experience of building numbers with base-ten materials on headed place value mats. They should record the numbers that they build. Pupils benefit from working with base-ten thousand cubes as well as with hundreds, tens and units blocks.

(ii) Teachers should target numbers such as 50, 400, 101, 2005, 3029 etc., making sure that dyslexic learners understand that an empty column is marked by a zero place-holder. Teachers should also make sure that pupils build the difficult 'teens' numbers and record them. Dyslexic pupils find it particularly confusing that, for example, 'thir' in the 'teen' number, thirteen, is said first, but recorded after the 1 in the written form, 13. Dyslexic learners frequently do better if they are permitted to write the 3 for 'thir', first, and then squeeze in the 1, to the right of the 3, afterwards.

(iii) Coins can further enhance place value understanding. An easily designed grid helps pupils understand '5-plus' ways of reasoning. From this, pupils easily progress onto tens and ones work.

Again pupils can see and record what happens each time that they add 10p.

From 6, count on 8 more.	Moving on to tens and units:
5p, 1p + 5p, 2p, 1p	From 15, count on 11 more.
$5p + 5p = 10p$	10p, 5p + 10p, 1p
and $2p + 1p + 1p = 4p$	$10p + 10p = 20p$
$10p + 4p = 14p$	and $5p + 1p = 6p$
	$20p + 6p = 26p$

(iv) Dyslexic pupils can also build numbers from ordinary digit cards or from overlay (arrow) cards. When using ordinary digit cards, the digits 1, 2 and 3 can be used to build the six numbers, 321, 312, 231, 213, 123 and 132.

(v) The grid of values up to HTU is straightforward. When higher values are reached, the grid of values is organised into classes of values with three in each: the class of ones (HTU); the class of thousands (Hundreds of thousands, Tens of thousands, Thousands); the class of millions, and so on. The basic HTU pattern is repeated:

$$\text{Millions} \ | \ \text{Thousands} \ | \ \text{Ones}$$
$$| \qquad\qquad |$$
$$\text{H T U} \ | \ \text{H T U} \ | \ \text{H T U}$$

(vi) The traditional, intermediate ThHTU model, in which there appears to be one kind of thousand only, often confuses pupils; many pupils develop a foreshortened mental model of the extended place value grid in which the one kind of thousands is next door to the millions position: MThHTU. From the beginning stages of working with thousands numbers, it is helpful to indicate the presence of the whole class of three values of thousands.

$$\text{Thousands} \ | \ \text{Ones}$$
$$|$$
$$\text{H T }\underline{\text{U}} \ | \ \mathbf{\underline{H} \ \underline{T} \ \underline{U}}$$

(vii) Many dyslexic pupils have difficulty reading very large numbers. It is time consuming to write detailed HTU headings above the individual digits. It is much more successful to encourage pupils to draw loops around the classes of three, starting with the class of ones. The drawn loops should always leave space for three values. For instance the thousands loop for 10 012 only has two of three possible digits in it, and it is read as ten thousand. In time, pupils learn to picture the loops of threes.

(a) $\widehat{23}\ \widehat{506}$; (b) $\widehat{1}\ \widehat{001}$; (c) $\widehat{406}\ \widehat{289}$; (d) $\widehat{1}\ \widehat{888}\ \widehat{777}$; (e) $\widehat{10}\ \widehat{000}\ \widehat{000}$;

(viii) It is useful to play games in which pupils earn units of value, for example +1, +10; +1, +10, +100 etc. Value units are accumulated on mats and each running total is recorded in headed place value columns beneath the previous total. Later on, pupils can play paper and pencil versions of place value spinner games.

A note on written decimal numbers

Decimal numbers are part of the overall decimal (tens-based, or base ten) system. It is an aid to dyslexic pupils if they are helped to extend their understanding of decimal numbers by placing them in the context of the place value grid. Three baguettes and two-tenths of a baguette, or three point two baguettes are:

$$HTU \quad \cdot \quad tenths \quad hundredths$$
$$3 \quad \cdot \quad 2$$

Some visually able dyslexics benefit from using renamed base-ten materials to understand decimal numbers.

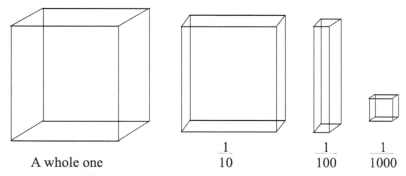

A whole one $\dfrac{1}{10}$ $\dfrac{1}{100}$ $\dfrac{1}{1000}$

Figure 3.1 Base-ten materials for decimal numbers.

Example	1.304 is bigger than	1.285
	1 block	1 block
	3 flats	2 flats
	no sticks	8 sticks
	4 cubes	5 cubes

Teaching calculation

Teaching facts

For all pupils, the key to acquiring a good foundation of known facts involves grasping that numbers are entities to be rearranged and mixed-and-matched so that the learner can figure out answers by thinking rather than by counting.

We have emphasised that many dyslexic pupils rely heavily on counting in calculation. For such pupils an over-reliance on counting undermines their ability to reason. This is because many dyslexic pupils cannot recall the most basic of the essential facts they must know. Instead, they frequently count to work out those facts which make all subsequent reasoning stages possible. Lack of basic maths facts knowledge then serves to perpetuate the counting habit. As we have seen, habitual counting undermines the ability of dyslexic pupils to acquire a growing body of known facts.

The sets of facts (key facts) which dyslexic pupils should know are:

(i)   the component pairs of facts of all the counting numbers to 9
(ii)   the facts of 10
(ii)   the addition doubles facts to $10 + 10$
(iv)   two tables facts in each sequence: $10 \times n$ and $5 \times n$.

Readily grasped, efficient and universal reasoning strategies include:

(i)   a components-based model of basic subtraction
(ii)   near-doubling in basic addition
(iii) a complementary addition reasoning approach in subtraction
(iv)   bridging-through-ten for larger through-ten additions and subtractions
(v)   a structured, efficient step-counting model of multiplication and division.

In a structured approach to learning maths facts:

- The essential facts to know (key facts) are learned first. The key facts are especially targeted for rehearsal and automatisation purposes.
- Each layer of facts (including the key facts) is rehearsed through reasoning to figure the facts out.
- All figuring out routes are initially modelled using concrete materials.
- Pupils rehearse efficient ways of figuring out selected facts from the whole body or set of facts to be learnt.
- Rehearsals set out to speed up the figuring-out process; they also set out to support/reinforce an ongoing process of automatisation.
- In time, rehearsals mix the targeted set of facts with other already learnt facts.
- Rehearsals or over-learning sessions include oral question-and-answer sessions; carefully designed, short written exercises; and simple games for which facts have to be figured out.

- Because dyslexic pupils frequently struggle to remember what they have learned, over-learning and automatisation can be facilitated and speeded up by the consistent and carefully monitored use of sets of rehearsal cards (rehearsal cards are described on page 31).

The basic building blocks of calculation: the component pairs of facts of the counting numbers to nine and the facts of ten

Many teachers believe that the basic addition facts are the foundation facts in maths. In fact, a great deal of subsequent reasoning in maths depends on a sound knowledge of the internal number bonds (or part-whole combinations) of all of the counting numbers to ten. The ability to use reasoning strategies is compromised whenever pupils do not have efficient access to all of the ways in which the basic numbers to ten can be broken down (decomposed).

For this reason, it is important for teachers to devote sufficient time to structured partitioning-of-numbers work. It is recommended that partitioning work is a main focus of early maths work with younger dyslexic learners. Teachers of older dyslexic pupils can usually feed basic components work, in subtle and unobtrusive ways, into a more advanced teaching programme.

One efficient way of helping dyslexic pupils to internalise the whole set of component facts of the numbers to nine, as well as the facts of ten, is to introduce them to a set of easily visualised number patterns. In addition to fostering number-sense, the number pattern model provides pupils with a core set of easy-to-visualise key component facts.

The set of number patterns, which works well with dyslexic pupils of all ages, makes use of symmetrical doubles patterns, near-doubles patterns and well-known dice/domino patterns.

Figure 3.2 Dice/domino patterns.

It is best if pupils have the experience of using small ones to construct the larger number patterns from the two equal or nearly equal parts that each of the quantities can be split into.

The set of number patterns can be made very familiar by:

(a) Drawing the patterns on blank cards or blank dice and using them in simple games (such as *Snap, Snakes and Ladders* etc.);
(b) Drawing the patterns on wall charts/posters;
(c) Integrating the patterns into basic worksheet exercises, and so on.

The ability to picture the number patterns enables pupils to know that, for example, 8 equals 4 plus 4, 9 equals 5 plus 4 and 10 equals 5 plus 5. Colloquial, action-based language helps to make this work transparent and accessible to younger pupils, for example 'What is the special pattern of nine built from?', 'What is the pattern of ten made of ?'

Some dyslexic pupils respond particularly well to the triad method of recording and presenting component facts:

Figure 3.3 Triad method of recording.

Once pupils are familiar with the number patterns, they can then be used to help pupils to visualise a key or foundation layer of missing addend components. In early work with younger pupils, teachers can cover the relevant part of the number pattern. The pupil has to figure out what is under the cover, for example:

'I have the pattern of 7 here, but we can only see 3. 7 is 'made of ' 3 and . . .?'
'Think of the pattern of 7. 7 is built from 4 and . . .?'
'The number 7 is made of 3 and . . .?'
3 + ___ = 7

Figure 3.4 Missing addend.

Once the missing addend facts are well known, the number patterns can also be used to figure out subtraction answers. This introduces pupils to a components-based model of basic subtraction in which no counting is involved. For example:

(a) The pattern of 9 is built from 5 and . . .? If you subtract 5, you are left with . . .?

(b) $9 - 5 = ?$, 9 is made of 5 and 4. If you subtract 5, you are left with 4.

Many grasshopper/older dyslexic pupils are able to generalise from their ability to visualise the set of facts, which the number patterns represent, to answer all of the other missing addend and basic subtraction facts.

On the other hand, where dyslexic pupils require further structured work on the component facts, the number patterns can be used to provide two useful starting points for reasoning. Because they are symmetrical and therefore easy to visualise, it is usually best to target the even number patterns, first.

The key doubles or near-doubles facts provide one starting point for reasoning. For example, in work on the number pattern of 6, pupils can reason, 'We know that 3 plus 3 equals 6, so 4 plus 2 equals 6'. Younger dyslexic pupils frequently respond very well to the colloquial formulation, 3 needs 3 to build 6, so 4 needs 2 to build 6. To work out $6 - 4$, pupils reason, 6 is made up of 4 and 2 so 6 subtract 4 is 2.

The outer edge facts provide the second starting point for reasoning. For example, when the number pattern of 8 is studied, pupils can see that '1 plus 7 is 8' is an easy fact to know; from there pupils can reason 'so 2 plus 6 equals 8'. Likewise, '7 plus 1 is 8' is an easy fact to know; therefore 6 plus 2 equals 8. To figure out $8 - 6$, pupils reason, 8 is made of 6 and 2 so 8 subtract 6 is 2.

The facts of ten

The base-ten structure of the number system provides a useful framework for a great deal of reasoning in maths. This means that the component facts of ten prove to be an extremely important set of facts to know. The number pattern of ten can be used to structure reasoning about ten. However, many dyslexic pupils benefit from working with a second linear model of ten (and, indeed, of the other counting numbers, too). Once again, the mid-point key fact, together with the outermost facts, are used to structure reasoning.

Subtraction from ten, using the components-based subtraction model, should be rehearsed as frequently as the missing addend facts of ten. For example: $10 - 4 = ?$, 10 is made of 4 and 6, so if you take away 4, you are left with 6. It is the ability to subtract from 10 that makes it possible for dyslexic pupils to figure out mental subtractions, such as $40 - 4$, efficiently, and subtraction from 10 is a key step in mental subtraction calculations, such as $13 - 5$ and $23 - 7$.

Many dyslexic students who have not received structured maths tuition go onto secondary school still using very basic counting strategies. This is partly because they are reluctant to move on from something that has given them correct answers in the past.

The facts of ten are a good place to start the necessary foundation work to introduce secondary school pupils to models of reasoning that are not counting-based. (The following work can also provide useful over-learning exercises for primary school dyslexic learners.)

The first step is to ask the pupil which numbers make ten when you add them together. Possible responses include:

(i)   The pupil may not know and will need to count on to find the answers. The number patterns, a bead string, or 5p and 1p coins can be used to reinforce the conservation of 10.

(ii) The pupil may know some of the bonds, for example $5 + 5$ or $9 + 1$. Other bonds may be reinforced using a Look and Cover technique.

(iii) The pupil may know all but one or two bonds, for example $7 + 3$. Use flash cards of bonds up to ten to pick out all pairs which make 10.

(iv) The pupil may know them all instantly. Move on to subtraction from ten, using flash cards.

   (a) Check 'Make 10' bonds in multiple additions to show that strategies can be applied to make their calculations quicker, for example $6 + 7 + 3 + 5 + 14$:

   $$14 + 6 = 20, \quad 7 + 3 = 10, \quad 20 + 10 = 30, \quad \text{then} + 5 = 35$$

   (b) Use 'Make 10' bonds in early algebra work or missing numbers to make ten, $9 + x = 10$

This work also helps some pupils understand almost ten, or compensation strategies (see page 61).

$9 + 6$ is almost $10 + 6$ which is 16 and $16 - 1 = 15$
$59 + 38$ is nearly $60 +$ nearly 40 which is 100, take away 1 (for 59) and 2 (for 38), which is 97.

'Make 10' bonds can be reinforced at each stage by playing the 'Make 10 Game', essentially a memory/pairs game. Work can be extended to 'Make 20' and then to 'Make 100'. Pupils are encouraged to use knowledge of the bonds of ten.

Doubling and near-doubling in figuring out addition facts

To ten

The doubles facts to 5 plus 5 are easily visualised by most pupils and are powerful patterns to exploit in reasoning. With concrete support, most dyslexic pupils understand the relatively simple near-doubling logic. For example, to figure out 4 plus 5, the pupil can reason, 4 plus 4 is 8, so 4 plus 5 is 9.

oooo   ooooo 4 + 5

oooo   oooo   4 + 4

oooo   oooo• 4 + 4 within 4 + 5

Once again, the triad form is a useful way of recording and supporting concrete work.

$4 + 5 = 8 + 1 = 9$

④   ①

To twenty

The doubles facts from 6 + 6 to 10 + 10 are a very useful set of facts for pupils to know. In reasoning rehearsals, the two easy facts, 5 plus 5 equals 10 and 10 plus 10 equals 20, can be used as the key facts. A pyramid model of doubles facts helps pupils to understand that each larger doubles step is two larger than the step before and that each smaller doubles step is two less than the step before. Thus to figure out 7 + 7, pupils reason, 5 plus 5 is 10, so 6 plus 6 is 12, and 7 plus 7 is 14. To figure out 9 + 9, pupils reason, 10 plus 10 is 20, so 9 plus 9 is 18.

Dyslexic pupils who have automatised the doubles facts to 20 generally use near-doubling strategies successfully to figure out through-ten facts such as 7 + 8 and 7 + 9, 7 + 6 and 7 + 5.

Preparing the way for success in subtraction

Dyslexic pupils find it hard to count backwards and have difficulty managing the double sequential demands and working memory burden of conventional counting-back subtraction methods. A components model of basic subtraction does not rely on counting. In all harder subtraction work, it is both easier and safer for dyslexic pupils to learn to reason forwards rather than to persist in counting backwards. The early stages of reasoning forwards in subtraction is often called 'counting up'. More advanced forms of reasoning forwards in subtraction are usually called complementary addition strategies. Dyslexic pupils benefit from early and ongoing work to build a flexible and efficient model of subtraction.

The habit of reasoning forwards in subtraction can be established in two complementary ways:

(i)   by broadening the dyslexic pupil's conceptual understanding of subtraction
(ii)   by modelling taking away on a line or track through working forwards from *one*, rather than backwards from the larger number.

The diverse concepts of subtraction

Comparisons between numbers and the missing addend concept

Subtraction is not just taking away. Subtraction is the operation that is involved in comparing two numbers, as well. The exercise of comparing two numbers breaks down into two related concepts: the concept of equalising two numbers, and the concept of finding the difference between two numbers. Dyslexic pupils generally find abstract comparisons of numbers very difficult to understand. Compare situations should be modelled concretely first; both of the numbers to be compared should be represented and they should be represented in easy to compare one-to-one correspondence. The equalising concept, which involves the concept and action of making the numbers equal, is easier to understand than the rather more abstract concept of difference, and should also be presented to pupils before the difference concept. It is also helpful to situate early compare work in terms of fair and unfair real-life situations.

Concrete Comparisons	Abstract Comparisons
We both have 5 chocolates: ●●●●● ●●●●●	We both start with the number 5.
Now I have 8 chocolates.　●●●●●○○○	Now I have 8 and you have 5.
You still have only 5.　●●●●●	

Equalising:

How many more chocolates do you need so that you have 8 chocolates too?	You want to reach 8. How many do you need?

Difference

How many more chocolates do I have than you?	How much bigger is 8 than 5?

The operation of subtraction also includes the missing addend concept, which is the concept that underlies a components-based model of subtraction. Presenting missing addend situations in real-life contexts and in terms of concrete linear number models helps to foster additional subtraction flexibility. In contrast to compare linear models, missing addend questions are modelled by building one line (or track).

Concrete missing addend	Abstract missing addend
My mum promised me 8 chocolates, but she only gave me 5 chocolates.	My target is the number 8. So far I have 5. How far is it from 5 to 8?

●●●●●○○○

How many chocolates must my mum give me (to keep her promise)?

Taking away, starting from one
Dyslexic pupils frequently need to be given explicit and concrete teaching in order to make sense of the easy-to-execute counting up

and complementary addition models of subtraction. Yet again, real-life contexts help to bring the notion of thinking forwards (rather than backwards) in subtraction to life.

You have a box of 8 of your favourite chocolate buttons.

•• •• •• ••

Your dad steals and eats the first 6 of your chocolate buttons. How many chocolate buttons are left?

xxxxxx•• •

Six chocolate buttons are gone, number 7 and number 8 are left, so 2 chocolate buttons are left.

Abstract counting up to models of 8 – 6 include the following: We start with 8. Then everything to the number 6 disappears. How many are left?

xxxxx 7 8

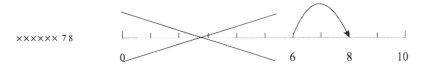

Figure 3.5 Linear model of counting up to.

2 are left.

Hard addition and subtraction facts: the universal bridging through ten strategy

The bridging through ten way of thinking, in which pupils use the ways that larger numbers are structured and reason to ten in a first step, allows pupils to figure out a wide range of calculations, for example:

In addition: 8 + 6, 36 + 6, 98 + 6
In subtraction: 13 – 5, 13 – 9; 42 – 6; 103 – 8

To use all bridging through ten strategies effectively, pupils need to have efficient knowledge of the facts of ten and of all the component facts of the other counting numbers to nine.

To use bridging back through ten strategies successfully, dyslexic pupils have to have confident knowledge of single-digit subtractions to the tens boundaries, for example 13 – 3 = 10; 42 – 2 = 40; 103 – 3 = 100. To execute the larger number through ten subtractions efficiently, pupils need to be able to subtract from the decade numbers, for example 40 – 6. To do this, dyslexic pupils need to understand that each decade is a ten. With this understanding, the figuring out process can start with the knowledge that 10 subtract 6 is 4, so 40 subtract 6 is 34.

Bridging in addition

To figure out 8 + 6, 8 is made up to 10 by splitting 6 into 2 + 4 and the 4 is then added to the 10 to make 14.

8 + 6

●●●●●●●●○○ ○○○○○○○○○○

+   ●● ●●●●

In these simple models, 8 is placed on a simple tens-structured track to 20. Pupils see that 8 needs 2 from the 6 to reach the 10; 6 is made of 2 and 4, so 4 remains to be added. 10 plus 4 is 14.

To figure out 36 + 8, 36 is made up to 40 by splitting the 8 into 4 + 4 and the 4 is then added to 40 to make 44.

A tens-structured bead string, a bead frame abacus or a simple track constructed from base-ten material (or Cuisinaire rods) can be used to model larger number bridging. At first, dyslexic pupils frequently benefit from structured number line support.

Figure 3.6 Bridging with number line.

Additional support is provided by the triad method of recording the figuring out process.

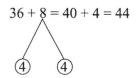

36 + 8 = 40 + 4 = 44

Bridging in subtraction

Bridging backwards to tens

To figure out 13 – 5, pupils subtract 3 from 13 to reach 10, and then subtract 2 from 10, which leaves 8.

13 – 5

●●●●●●●●●●   ●●●○○○○○○○

–   ○○   ○○○

13 is placed on a simple structured track to 20. To subtract 5 from 13, the 3 is subtracted or removed first.

●●●●●●●●●●   ○○○○○○○○○

The further 2 (from the 5) is then subtracted and removed from the 10, leaving 8.

●●●●●●●●○○   ○○○○○○○○○

To figure out 42 – 6, pupils subtract from 2 from 42 to reach 40, and then subtract 4 from 40, which leaves 36. Once again, tools such as a tens-structured bead string, a bead frame abacus, or a track, which has been constructed from base-ten materials, can be used to model larger number bridging back strategies. Mental calculation rehearsals of examples such as 42 – 6 may be supported by the use of tens-structured number lines.

Figure 3.7 Bridging backwards using a number line.

Bridging forwards to tens

To figure out calculations such as 13 – 9, where the number to be subtracted (the minuend) is large, and is therefore close to the start-out number (the subtrahend), pupils reason forwards from 9 to 10, which is 1, and then from 10 to 13, which is 3. The 1 and 3 are added together: 1 + 3 = 4; 13 – 9 = 4.

In essence, reasoning forwards to and beyond ten in through-ten subtraction work is a complementary addition strategy. To prepare the way for successful bridging forwards through ten work, dyslexic pupils should first solve through ten equalising problems, through ten difference problems, and through ten missing addend problems. Dyslexic pupils should also review the idea of taking away starting from one.

13 – 9

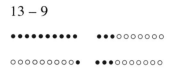

13 is placed on a simple tens-structured track to 20. Starting from one, 9 is removed from the first decade (or ten). Pupils see that 1 remains to 10, and that 3 remain, between 10 and 13.

Early mental rehearsals of subtraction calculations, such as 13 – 9, can be supported using a tens-structured number line:

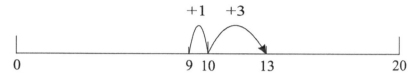

Figure 3.8 Bridging forwards on a number line.

Multiplication and division work

In order to reason effectively in multiplication and division work, dyslexic pupils first need to have a good understanding of the ways in which groups function as entities or units in calculation. Before the tables sequences are tackled, it is important to engage in practical work with groups.

Counting groups

Dyslexic pupils benefit from practice at step-counting in multiples of 2, 5, 3, 4 and 6. They should be encouraged to use concrete materials, a few times at least, to build the sequences of multiples. Coins can be used to practise counting in multiples of 2, 5 and 10. Using materials helps to ensure that dyslexic pupils understand that step-counting is basically multiple addition of the same group, over and over again. Because dyslexics typically struggle to remember aural/verbal sequential patterns, they often rely quite heavily on addition (and subtraction) skills in step-counting.

Dyslexic pupils should practise step-counting the easy multiples forwards and backwards from a variety of different starting points. They should also practise step-counting short ways to generate sequences of multiples of 7, 8 and 9. Teachers need to ensure that pupils are able to execute bridging additions and subtractions efficiently; for example, 36 + 6, 48 + 8; 54 – 6, 72 – 8 (see page 47). Teachers should also ensure that pupils are able to subtract single digits from decade numbers for example 60 – 6, 70 – 7, 80 – 8, etc. (see page 42).

To pave the way for efficient figuring out skills, dyslexic pupils should practise step-counting one or two steps forwards or backwards from a given multiple, and especially from the key tables multiples. For example, 'What number is two threes more than 15?' and 'What number is two threes less than 30?'

'Building' groups: multiplication and division

In building activities, teachers use simple, transparent language to ask pupils to build small numbers of groups from concrete ones. For example, 'Using these counters, can you build three groups of four? Count in fours so that you can figure out how many counters you have used'.

Figure 3.9 Building groups.

Building groups as patterns helps dyslexic pupils to visualise the groups.

The grouping concept of division is much more accessible than the sharing concept of division. Dyslexic pupils become confident about the operation of division if they practise grouping in early foundation-building division work. Teachers ask pupils to build groups from a given quantity to figure out simple division questions. Again, teachers should use simple activity-based language. 'Here are 20 counters. How many fives can you build from 20 counters?'

Abstract work: visualising groups to figure out multiplication and division facts

At first, dyslexic pupils make best progress if teachers make sure they use transparent, colloquial language:

'How many in four groups of five'?

'You have 15. How many threes can you build out of 15?'

In time, teachers need to introduce increasingly abstract multiplicative language. For example, 'What is four times four?' and 'How many sixes are there in 18?'

A simple, universal tables strategy

Dyslexic pupils benefit from learning and rehearsing a simple, universal tables and division strategy. Each individual tables sequence should be studied in turn. Once individual tables sequences have been mastered, pupils should be asked to generate out-of-sequence tables and division facts from more than one sequence. Because the universal tables and division strategy applies to all of the tables sequences, many dyslexic pupils realise that they can use their knowledge of how the strategy works to figure out the answers in a new sequence for themselves. Many dyslexic pupils also use additional helpful patterns to generate tables facts, for example, they remember that $4 \times n$ can be worked out by doubling $2 \times n$. Because of their long-term memory difficulties, most dyslexic pupils need to revisit tables and division work at regular intervals. Rehearsal cards (see page 31) help dyslexic pupils with the process of automatising the key tables facts. Rehearsal cards can also be used to allow for daily rehearsals of any individual tables facts that a pupil has difficulty figuring out.

In early work to understand the tables and division strategy, dyslexic pupils should be encouraged to construct a concrete model of the targeted sequence. Dyslexic pupils may begin working to master any tables sequence. In practice, it is usually best to begin formal tables learning work by rehearsing an easily visualised and easily counted tables sequence.

In each tables sequence, there are two facts only which need to be automatised. These facts should be thoroughly rehearsed and regularly revisited. As we have noted, the two key tables facts, from which all of the harder tables facts can be derived, are $5 \times n$ and $10 \times n$. Concrete (or pictorial) models of the tables sequences should highlight the mid-point $5 \times n$ fact in some way. This helps dyslexic pupils understand that $5 \times n$ is half of $10 \times n$.

At the start of early tables and division exercises, pupils should be required to generate the two key tables; the key tables facts can be described as the easy-to-know facts which will help pupils to figure out the hard tables or division facts.

The tables and division strategy explained, using the × 5 tables sequence

The easy tables are known or step-counted from a known fact, for example $3 \times 5 = 2$ fives plus 5.

The harder facts are step-counted from the key facts, 5×5 or 10×5:

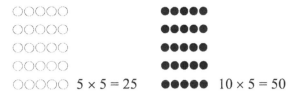

Figure 3.10 The five times tables sequence.

$6 \times 5 = (5 \times 5) + 5$. At first, pupils generally reason '5 times 5 is 25, so 6 times 5 is 30'. In time, pupils are encouraged to reason more efficiently: $(5 \times 5 = 25)$, 30.

7×5: $(5 \times 5) + 5 + 5 = 25, 30, 35$

9×5: $(10 \times 5) - 5 = 50 - 5$. Pupils reason back from 10×5. 9×5 is one five less than 10×5, so 9×5 'equals' 45.

4×5: Pupils step-count from 2×5 or 3×5; reason back from the key table, 5×5; or double 2×5.

8×5: Pupils can reason back from 10×5: $8 \times 5 = (10 \times 5 = 50)$ 45, 40. Some pupils perform better if they reason forwards from 5×5: $8 \times 5 = (5 \times 5 = 25)$ 30, 35, 40. Some able dyslexic pupils figure out $8 \times n$ as double $4 \times n$: $4 \times 5 = 20$ so $8 \times 5 = 40$.

Division questions should always be practised alongside multiplication questions. The key tables and the grouping model of division are used in the figuring out process. At first, transparent action-based language is used:

'How many fives would we need to 'build' 35 out of fives?'

'5 fives are 25, 6 fives are 30, and 7 fives are 35. We need 7 fives to build 35.'

In time, teachers should set out to use the more standard formulations, such as

'How many fives are there in 45?' or (later) 'What is 45 divided by 5?'

'10 fives are 50, so there are 9 fives in 45'.

Some important points to note

In early tables work, dyslexic pupils should be encouraged to record spoken tables facts and interpret written tables facts in consistent ways. It is usual, nowadays, to write 'three times four' as 3×4. It is also usual to interpret the symbolic 4×6 as four groups of six or four sixes. In the past, the times tables facts were recorded, and interpreted, the opposite way round. 'Three times five' was written as 5×3, and was understood as 'five multiplied by three', or 'five, multiplied three times'. Some textbooks still represent tables sequences this way. Pupils who are learning to make sense of multiplication and division can become muddled if they encounter different ways of representing tables facts and tables sequences.

Dyslexic pupils who are developing more confident and flexible interpretations of multiplication may well choose to interpret 6×3 as three groups of six. It helps if teachers make explicit that the pupil is choosing to think about sixes rather than threes: **6** × 3, rather than 6 × **3**. Likewise, teachers can also make explicit that a pupil is thinking about sevens, rather than eights, when he or she figures out 7×8 as $(7 \times 7) + 7$. Dyslexic pupils who use the commutative principle in a purely abstract or rule-led way often make reasoning mistakes: for instance, in the last example, they may add 8 to 7×7.

The sharing concept informs many division word problem situations. Dyslexic pupils can most easily grasp sharing in the context of solving simple real-life problems. For example, '15 large chocolates are shared fairly between 3 boys. How many chocolates does each boy get?' Concrete solutions should avoid the mechanical (and ultimately unhelpful) dealing cards or dealing ones model of sharing. Instead pupils should be encouraged to guess and check the size of the fair shares. Many dyslexic pupils enjoy drawing stick figures to allocate the fair shares to.

Calculation procedures: two-digit and three-digit calculations

As we have said, there is usually considered to be one correct way to carry out standard procedures, but there are a number of different ways to complete calculations using mental methods. As calculations become harder, many dyslexic pupils need to be encouraged to write down calculation steps. This is because they should not rely on their working memory to hold all of the partial calculations successfully. Grasshopper dyslexic learners tend to resist pressure to write things down but must be encouraged to do so.

The advantages of mental calculation methods for dyslexic pupils are that:

(a) mental calculations do not have to be set out in columns
(b) mental methods do not involve redistribution (carrying/ borrowing) difficulties.

Recommended universal calculation methods

In the early stages of calculating, dyslexic pupils benefit from using concrete objects, such as base-ten materials or Cuisenaire rods, to model the mental calculations that they are given to solve. They should explain what the problems mean and voice their solutions. Before dyslexic pupils are required to work abstractly, it often helps if they are asked to draw diagrams of the values that are present in the problem. Teachers should sequence the difficulty of calculation examples carefully. For instance, in short multiplication work, pupils should model and solve 'teens' calculations involving easy tables first, for example:

$3 \times 14 = 3$ groups of $14 = $ (10p 1p 1p 1p 1p) (10p 1p 1p 1p 1p) (10p 1p 1p 1p 1p) = 3 groups of ten, or thirty, and 3 groups of four, or twelve = $30 + 12 = 42$.

The following mental methods are accessible to dyslexic learners, including younger or less able learners. They are easy to model and execute and they do not require large amounts of working memory. They are good methods for 'in-the-head' calculations and are described in the NNS materials.

Partitioning

Partitioning methods can be used to solve two-digit and even three-digit addition, short and long multiplication calculations. Pupils work with the real values making up the numbers and the basic addition and multiplication facts apply. In other words, basic facts knowledge can be adapted to larger values, for example:

$4 \times 3 = $ (1p 1p 1p) (1p 1p 1p) (1p 1p 1p) (1p 1p 1p)

4×30 (3 tens) = (10p 10p 10p) (10p 10p 10p) (10p 10p 10p) (10p 10p 10p)

$4 \times 300 = $ (£1 £1 £1) (£1 £1 £1) (£1 £1 £1) (£1 £1 £1) [because £1 = 100p]

The partitioning model extends well to many larger number calculations, for example:

$35 + 28 = (30 + 5) + (20 + 8) = 50 + 13 = 63$

The numbers are 'chunked' into their component parts and each place value is calculated in turn. It is usual to start with the largest-value digits first, for example:

H   T   U

$367 + 58 = 300 + 110 + 15 = 425$ [adding the 100s, 10s and units separately first]
$5 \times 525 = 2500 + 100 + 25 = 2625$ [multiplying the 100s, 10s and units separately]

The most accessible mental model for long multiplication is also a partitioning model. In long multiplication calculations it is difficult for pupils to keep track of all of the component calculations. This method can help dyslexic pupils to do so.

The box model: for example, 17×18

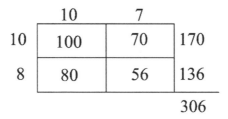

	10	7	
10	100	70	170
8	80	56	136
			306

Figure 3.11 Partitioning for multiplication.

Partitioning, or breaking down numbers into easy-to-manage component parts, is also a way of proceeding (or a mindset) which can help dyslexic pupils figure out a number of different kinds of calculations. A few examples include:

Money problems: $8 \times £4.69 = 8 \times £4 (= £32) + 8 \times 69 = 480 + 72$ $(= £5.52) = £37.52$

Fraction problems: $3\frac{1}{2} + 2\frac{1}{4} = 3 + 2(= 5) + \frac{1}{2} + \frac{1}{4} (= \frac{3}{4}) = 5\frac{3}{4}$

Decimal problems: $5.6 \times 4 = 5 \times 4 (= 20) + 0.6 \times 4 (= 2.4) = 22.4$

Measurement problems: $2.35m + 80cm = 2m + 35cm + 80cm$ $(= 1.15m) = 3.15m$

Learning to double and halve numbers is important. Reasoning from the 5 and 10 times tables facts, linked with the role of 10, makes many calculations possible. For example:

352×27 is 352×20 and 352×7

352×20 is $(352 \times 2) \times 10$

For 352×2:

Double 300, 50 and 2 is $600 + 100 + 4 = 704$

So, $352 \times 20 = 704 \times 10$ $= 7040$

For 352×7:

300×7 is $3 \times 100 \times 7$

$\quad = (3 \times 100 \times 5) + (3 \times 100 \times 2)$

$\quad = (15 \times 100) + (6 \times 100)$

$\quad = 21 \times 100$ $= 2100$

50×7 is $5 \times 10 \times 7$

$\quad = 35 \times 10$ $= 350$

2×7 $= \underline{14}$

9504

Sequencing

Sequencing methods are recommended for larger-number subtractions. Some pupils choose a sequencing method to solve certain addition calculations. The hallmark of sequencing methods is that pupils begin calculating from one of the whole numbers in the problem, for example:

$35 + 28 = 35 + 20 + 8 = 55 + 8 = 63$

In sequencing work, concrete number tracks are the most useful concrete tools for pupils to use. Structured, emptier number lines, and empty number lines, give dyslexic pupils useful working memory support in subtraction work. The empty number line model features in the Numeracy Strategy and in many newer textbooks.

The empty number line concept is quite abstract and is not automatically understood by dyslexic pupils. It is recommended that they have a gradual introduction to it. First, pupils should record the sequential calculation steps, which can be physically demonstrated on concrete number tracks, onto easier to understand structured emptier number lines; once pupils are familiar with the idea of recording calculation steps as drawn loops on a line, they can be introduced to the empty number line model.

In sequencing subtraction models, pupils either

(i) start from the bigger number (the minuend) and reason backwards in sequential steps: $30 - 17$: $30 - 10 = 20$; $20 - 7 = 13$

(ii) start from the smaller number (the subtrahend) and reason forwards in sequential steps: 30 − 17: (17) + 3 (to 20) + 10 (to 30); 3 + 10 = 13

Sequencing back

This is the mental subtraction model which most dyslexic pupils intuitively choose to solve subtraction calculations. This model works well for subtraction from round numbers. However, working memory difficulties can contribute to a common calculation error. In the second calculation step, dyslexic pupils frequently add, whereas they should continue to subtract. To solve 100 − 64, for example, dyslexic pupils frequently say 'A hundred take away sixty is forty, forty plus four is forty-four.' Using real-life situations, together with a supportive cognitive model, helps many dyslexic pupils to iron out this calculation bug, for example: 'You have 50 chocolates. Your brother steals and eats 34 of your chocolates. How many chocolates do you have, now?'

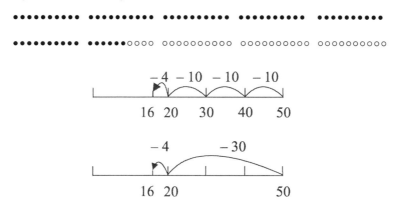

Figure 3.12 Sequencing back for subtraction.

The sequencing back method is quite hard to use in trying to figure out non-rounded calculations, such as 53 − 27, and it is especially hard to use when the bigger number is greater than 100. This is because the first part of the calculation is tricky and requires a great deal of working memory. For example, in the calculation 134 − 76, the first step is the rather difficult 134 − 70.

As long as pupils are generally encouraged to reason, rather than count in ones, an ordinary number line, or ruler, can be used to support sequencing subtraction work and also prepare the way for understanding negative numbers. On a ruler, the full range of numbers is visible to students and the value 0 can be seen.

8 − 3: Find 8, count back 3 = 5.

26 − 14: Find 26, subtract 10 to 16 then back 4 more to 12,

or find 26, subtract 4 to 22 then back 10 more to 12.

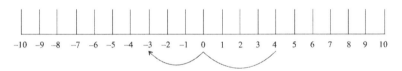

4 − 7: Find 4, count back 7 = − 3, or 7 is made up of 4 + 3 so go back 4 to 0 and 3 more to − 3.

If a metre rule is used, counting back from one hundred in tens and units is possible (thousands if you count the millimetres!).

More sequencing back calculation examples:

Money: £5.00 − £3.75: £5.00 − £3.00 = £2.00; £2.00 − 75p = £1.25

Fractions: $6 - 2\frac{3}{4}$: 6 − 2 = 4; $4 - \frac{3}{4} = 3\frac{1}{4}$

Decimals: 10 − 7.8: 10 − 7 = 3; 3 − 0.8 = 2.2

Measurements: 4 litres − 2 litres 645 ml: 4 l − 2 l = 2 l; 2 l − 645 ml = 1 l 355 ml

Sequencing forwards: complementary addition

All pupils find subtraction calculations more difficult than addition calculations. As we have seen, dyslexic pupils have particular difficulty with sequential processes which proceed backwards. We have also noted many times that complementary addition procedures are the safest subtraction procedures to use because the calculation steps are relatively easy to execute and do not require too much working memory. Complementary addition is the best mental model to use to solve calculations such as 57 − 34 and 134 − 36.

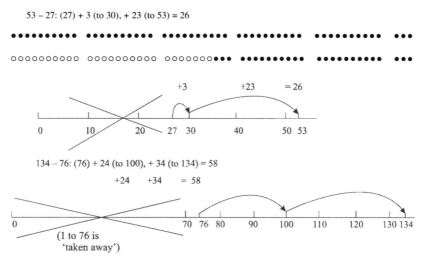

53 − 27: (27) + 3 (to 30), + 23 (to 53) = 26

134 − 76: (76) + 24 (to 100), + 34 (to 134) = 58

Figure 3.13 Complementary addition for subtraction.

Ordinary number lines (rulers/metre rules) can also be used to support counting on in tens and ones. Number lines can be used for counting on in decimals.

Some teaching tips:

(i) Two-digit comparison (or compare) work and missing addend work helps prepare the way for larger number complementary addition work.
(ii) Pupils can work with money to give change 'the shopkeeper's way'.
(iii) Numbers which are close together should be selected at first, for example, 53 − 49; 134 − 128, then numbers which are further apart.
(iv) Before subtractions from numbers which are greater than 100 are tackled, rehearse subtractions from 100 in mental maths practice sessions.

More complementary addition subtraction examples:

Time: How many hours and minutes between 2:35 p.m. and 6:05 p.m: (2:35 p.m.) + 25 min (to 3 o' clock); (3 o' clock) + 3 h 5 min (to 6:05) = 3 h 30 min

Angles: 180 − 97: (97) + 3 (to 100); (100) + 80 (to 180) = 83

Fractions: $4\frac{1}{3} - 1\frac{2}{3} = (1\frac{2}{3}) + \frac{1}{3}$ (to 2); (2) + $2\frac{1}{3}$ (to $4\frac{1}{3}$) = $2\frac{2}{3}$

Decimals: 13.5 − 8.9 = (8.9) + 1.1 (to 10); (10) + 3.5 (to 13.5) = 4.6

Measurement: 5 kg 67 g − 3 kg 875 g: (3 kg 875 g) + 125 g (to 4 kg); (4 kg) + 1 kg 67 g (to 5 kg 67 g) = 1 kg 192 g

Removing tens: short and long division

This is a grouping model of division, which can also be applied in solving sharing problems. In the removing tens division approach, pupils proceed by building up, and subtracting, large multiples of the divisor (the number that pupils are required to divide by). The model can be used to solve both short and long division calculations. In the removing tens approach to division, the reasoning steps are transparent enough for most dyslexic pupils to follow. This means that pupils are able to execute the necessary sequence of steps with understanding. Pupils can choose to work with smaller or larger multiples of the divisor, depending on their mental multiplication skills. Most dyslexic pupils develop the ability and confidence to work with larger multiples. This means that most dyslexic pupils are able to execute short and long division calculations with growing efficiency.

Figure 3.14 Removing tens for division.

Compensation

It should be noted that compensation methods (in which pupils overshoot or undershoot in the first step, and then adjust the calculation afterwards) are not universal methods. They do not apply equally well to all numbers. They are suitable for more able pupils. For example, 35 + 28 ≈ 35 + 30 = 65; 65 − 2 = 63. [subtract 2 to compensate]

The pervasiveness of multiplication and division by 10, 100 and 1000

$3 \times 10 = 30$ $3 \times 100 = 300$ $3 \times 1000 = 3000$

$32 \times 10 = 320$ $32 \times 100 = 3200$ $32 \times 1000 = 32\,000$

$32 \times 20 = 32 \times 2 \times 10 = 640$ etc.

$60 \times 300 = 6 \times 3 \times 10 \times 100 = 18\,000$

$50 \div 10 = 5$ $500 \div 10 = 50$ $4380 \div 10 = 438$

$3400 \div 100 = 34$ $560\,000 \div 1000 = 560$

$350 \div 70 = (350 \div 7) \div 10 = 50 \div 10 = 5$ etc.

$\dfrac{1}{10}$ of $120 = 12$ $\dfrac{1}{1000}$ of $67\,000 = 67$

Percentages: 20% of $380 = 20 \times 380 \div 100 = 7600 \div 100 = 76$

Decimals: $3.16 \times 10 = 31.6$ $6.80 \times 100 = 680$
    $13.2341 \times 1000 = 13234.1$

Jane buys 10 sweets at 5p each. How much does she spend?
$10 \times 5p = 50p$

Fred spends £360 on 30 CDs. How much would one cost him on average? £360 ÷ 30 = £12

Measure: Convert 600 cm into metres: $600 \div 100 = 6$ m

Convert 6 litres into millilitres: $6 \times 1000 = 6000$ ml

Scales: 1:25 000, so 4 cm represents $4 \times 25\,000 = 100\,000$ cm = 100 km

Standard form: $500 = 5 \times 10^2$

Rounding to the nearest 10, 100, 1000

Area and volume: $l = 20$, $w = 40$, Area = $20 \times 40 = 800$ square units
       $l = 30$, $w = 10$, $h = 60$, Volume = $30 \times 10 \times 60 = 18\,000$ cubic units

The standard calculation procedures: sums in columns

Generally speaking, the standard calculation procedures are the most efficient procedures to use when calculations can be written down and when large numbers are involved. Pupils in state primary school classrooms learn the standard procedures from about the end of Year 3 onwards. In many independent schools, the standard column methods of calculating are the first calculation methods that pupils learn when they begin working with large numbers, and later some mental methods may be taught in order to foster the mental proficiency of pupils.

We have seen that a large proportion of dyslexic pupils find it difficult to remember how to complete the standard procedures. Many dyslexic pupils make errors demonstrating a lack of important conceptual understandings. The redistribution concepts are particularly difficult to understand. As the standard procedures are structured in very abstract and analytical ways, they frequently feel counter-intuitive to grasshopper dyslexic learners.

To help dyslexic pupils learn the standard procedures, it is advisable that they have some experience of using base-ten materials to model the steps of the procedures. Materials should be placed on headed mats, in the relevant columns, and then moved, as necessary, as the standard steps are followed through. Pupils should be encouraged to voice the steps they are executing. They should also record the calculation steps in the standard written forms.

A teaching tip for the standard subtraction procedure

The error which dyslexic pupils commonly make in standard column subtraction is that they fail to borrow (or decompose) in situations in which this is necessary. Instead, dyslexic pupils illegitimately flip the digits within a column, and subtract the smaller number from the larger number. As well as ensuring that pupils understand the concept and process of decomposition, it is helpful to clarify, and have pupils voice correctly, subtractions, such as $2 - 6$, and $0 - 6$. This is because dyslexic pupils frequently describe basic subtraction questions incorrectly, translating $6 - 2$ as '2 take away 6', but then actually subtract 2 from 6. In addition to this, many dyslexic pupils internalise the pragmatic but ultimately misleading rule that you always look for the bigger number in subtraction and then subtract from that number. Primary school dyslexic pupils need to understand that, when you are working with ordinary numbers, if you only have two counters, it is not possible to take away six counters. However, secondary school dyslexic pupils might need to review the concept of negative numbers in the context of thinking about subtractions such as $2 - 6$ or $0 - 6$.

Informal column procedures

There are organisational and working memory advantages involved in setting out large/complex calculations in a column format because this means that the different values in the calculation are grouped together. Some dyslexic pupils find it hard to adjust to the idea that the standard procedural rules, for all operations, except for division, require calculating from the smallest place value first. In directional terms, the standard procedures generally require that pupils proceed, step-by-step, from right to left, whereas, mental strategies generally proceed in a right-to-left direction.

It is sometimes a help to dyslexic pupils if they are taught to employ non-standard mental calculation procedures, within the framework of the standard columns. Like all mental calculation methods, the advantage of low stress (Thompson, 1999) calculation methods is that redistribution skills are not required. Teaching experience has shown that a number of dyslexic pupils are able to adjust to the more economical standard methods, after they have used the low stress procedures. Base-ten materials can be used to clarify the fact that standard procedures do not involve calculations with the real values of numbers but rather involve working with units-of-value within the place value structure.

Examples of low stress methods include:

87	306	35
+ 58	− 187	× 6
130 (80 +50)	13 (to 200)	180 (6 × 30)
15 (7 + 8)	106 (to306)	30 (6 × 5)
145	119	210

An addition partitioning game that paves the way for formal addition

In the *Tens and Units* game, pupils have to reach a given number by using a spinner to pick up tens or units blocks. This helps pupils understand place value and adding tens.

26　　+　　32

T	U
○ ○	○○○○○○
○ ○ ○	○ ○
5	8

The answer is 58 and moving to algorithm is natural!

This game also helps pupils understand carrying conventions.

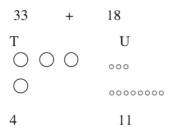

33　　　+　　　18

4　　　　　　　11

Exchange 10 units for 1 ten

4 + 1　　　　1

5　　　　　　1

The answer is 51.

Calculator use

The use of a calculator has to be taught to dyslexic pupils. Pupils who use mental methods might find aspects of calculator work problematic, as their methods will not easily relate to the function buttons available to them. The language of maths needs to be explored so that pupils can work out which buttons to press. For example, to find 20% of 360, it helps to ask 'What does per cent mean?' Per cent means 'out of 100'. So 20% means 20 out of 100. How do we put this into the calculator? We divide: 20 ÷ 100 = 0.2. Now we multiply by 360 because in 20% of 360, 'of' means 'times': 0.2 × 360 = 72.

Basic fraction work

Fractions are often very confusing for dyslexic pupils. This is because many of them find it difficult to visualise the different fractional forms and have great difficulty maintaining a grasp of the part-whole relationships which are involved. Also, as we have noted, many dyslexics have difficulty with the language used in naming the fractional forms and with the special vocabulary associated with fractions (top-heavy/improper fractions, mixed numbers etc.). Finally, fractions do not seem to follow the rules that apply to whole numbers. For instance as the bottom (denominator) of the fraction gets bigger, the value of the fraction decreases.

Suggestions for building a basic conceptual understanding of, and feel for, parts of wholes

Establishing an understanding of less than one, and one in fractional parts

(1) Cutting and building activities

    (a) Select a representation of one (or a whole), which can be cut into parts. Coloured paper squares, or paper strips, or pieces of sliced bread, work well. Squares and strips could represent cakes and chocolate bars.

    (b) Carefully establish the vocabulary of the fractional forms, beginning with the most common forms, half/halves, thirds and quarters. Ask 'If we want to split this strip/chocolate bar into thirds, how many pieces must we cut it into?' and 'This square/cake is split into four parts, what are the parts called?'

    (c) Use a drawn outline of one to build up the fractional parts, from one part through to all the parts which equal one or one whole. Record the entire building process. For instance, $\frac{1}{4}, \frac{2}{4}, \frac{3}{4}$, and $\frac{4}{4}$, which equals one or one whole. Emphasise that when we write fractions the tops, or numerators, describe the number of parts of the whole which are represented (have been built/are shaded etc.), whereas the bottoms or denominators tell us how many parts the whole or one has been split into.

(2) Shading activities

    (a) Draw lines to split pictorial representations of squares, strips and circles into the common fractional parts, shade the parts one by one to build up to the whole, and record the building process: $\frac{1}{3}, \frac{2}{3}, \frac{3}{3}$, and $\frac{3}{3} = 1$.

    (b) Keep drawing attention to what a whole one is in terms of the particular fractional form that you are working with. For instance 'If you have split a chocolate bar into quarters/four parts and you have all four of the parts, what have you got?' '$\frac{4}{4} = ?$'

    (c) Introduce simple spoken real-life addition and subtraction situations, and ask pupils to record them. For example, 'Before supper, you ate $\frac{1}{3}$ of a chocolate bar. After supper you ate another $\frac{2}{3}$ of the chocolate bar. How much of the chocolate bar did you eat altogether?' $\frac{1}{3} + \frac{2}{3} = \frac{3}{3} = 1$. 'Your mum gave you a chocolate bar to eat after dinner. While you were eating your dinner, someone stole one-quarter of your chocolate bar. How much of your chocolate bar did you have left?' '1 $\left(\frac{4}{4}\right) - \frac{1}{4} = \frac{3}{4}$'. Set pupils similar number problems to solve, for example $\frac{1}{4} + \frac{2}{4} = ?$

(d) Engage in similar work with other fractional forms, such as fifths, sixths and tenths.

(3) Paper-folding activities

Paper-folding makes the role of the denominator clear because the more times you fold the paper, the more sections you get, and the smaller each piece is.

This can be demonstrated by folding pieces of paper.

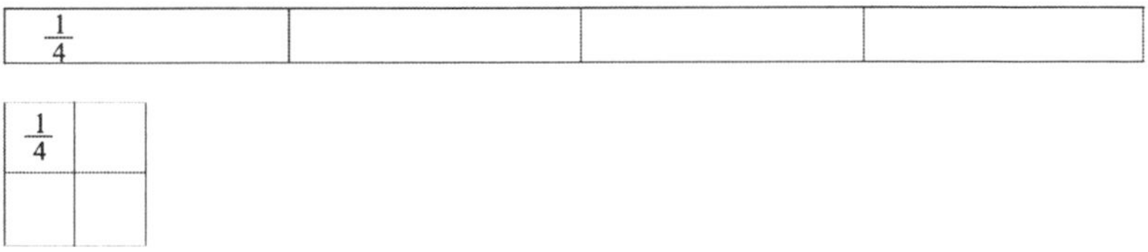

These shapes have been folded into 4 parts and each piece is one out of 4, $\frac{1}{4}$.

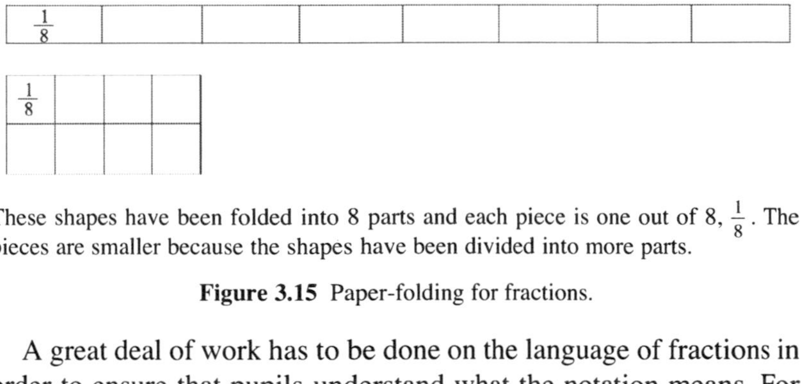

These shapes have been folded into 8 parts and each piece is one out of 8, $\frac{1}{8}$. The pieces are smaller because the shapes have been divided into more parts.

Figure 3.15 Paper-folding for fractions.

A great deal of work has to be done on the language of fractions in order to ensure that pupils understand what the notation means. For example, $\frac{2}{5}$ is 2 out of 5 parts, or the whole has been divided into 5 parts, and you want 2 of them. The phrases, 'out of' and 'divided into' are essential for pupils to understand when they move on to calculating with fractions.

Working to understand more than one in fractional terms

(1) Two (or more) concrete/pictorial/paper ones are split into a selected common fractional part, for example halves, thirds or

quarters. The building/shading process proceeds beyond one. The language forms for both mixed number representations and for top-heavy/improper fractional form representations are established: 'one-half', two halves or one, one and a half, two; one half, two halves or one, three halves, four halves, or two'.

(2) The practical work with more than one is recorded in the mixed number and top-heavy fraction forms. For example 3 split into thirds, and built back into wholes, is recorded as: $\frac{1}{3}, \frac{2}{3}, \frac{3}{3}$ or 1, $1\frac{1}{3}$, $1\frac{2}{3}$, $1\frac{3}{3}$ or 2, $2\frac{1}{3}$, $2\frac{2}{3}$, $2\frac{3}{3}$ or 3; $\frac{1}{3}, \frac{2}{3}, \frac{3}{3}$ (or 1), $\frac{4}{3}, \frac{5}{3}, \frac{6}{3}$ (or 2), $\frac{7}{3}, \frac{8}{3}, \frac{9}{3}$ (or 3).

(3) Introduce simple recorded real-life situations, followed by number problems, at this level. At first, it is helpful to select outcomes just bigger than one.

(a) You ate $\frac{3}{4}$ of a mini pizza. After drinking a glass of water, you ate another $\frac{2}{4}$ of a mini pizza. How much pizza did you eat altogether? $\frac{3}{4} + \frac{2}{4} = \frac{5}{4} = 1\frac{1}{4}$.

(b) $\frac{2}{3} + \frac{2}{3} = ?$

(c) $1\frac{2}{3} - \frac{1}{3} = ?$

(4) When dyslexic pupils are learning to work with more than one in fractional terms, it is also helpful to play a simple game. Two (or three) different fractional forms are selected, for example thirds and quarters. Each player generates fractional parts, for example by spinning a spinner. In this simple game, the possible fractional parts which players could generate include $\frac{1}{3}, \frac{2}{3}; \frac{1}{4}, \frac{2}{4}, \frac{3}{4}$. Each player also has a base containing drawn representations of a number of ones; some of the ones are split into thirds and an equal number of the ones are split into quarters. Each player takes it in turn to generate a fractional part and then shades the designated part on his/her base. The goal is to complete as many ones as possible. At any point in the game, a player may be asked to describe what he/she has accumulated in the selected fractional forms. This running total could be described as a mixed number or as a top-heavy fraction. Each player's final outcome is recorded in both mixed number and top-heavy fraction forms.

Basic decimal work

(1) Precede decimal work by working with fractional tenths in some of the ways described above.

(2) Introduce the decimal notational form as an alternative way of representing tenths. Keep drawing attention to one, and ones, in relation to decimal parts. For example: $\frac{10}{10} = 1$; $\frac{3}{10}$ is less than 1, and is written as 0.3. $1\frac{9}{10}$ is more than one, less than 2, is very close to 2 and is written 1.9. Draw attention to the $\frac{1}{2} = 0.5$ relationship. It is helpful to build a feel for decimals in relation to halves, as well as to wholes, for example 3.6 is just bigger than $3\frac{1}{2}$.

(3) Introduce measurement as one classic way of using decimals. It is helpful to engage in practical measurement activities, and record them. For example a pencil measures 7 cm 4 mm, or 7.4 cm. The pupil measures approximately 1 m and 3 parts of a metre, or 1.3 m. Alternatively, given lengths can be constructed: a dinosaur measures 4.6 m, in length: to show this, requires 4 whole metre sticks, and an additional 0.6 of a metre stick.

(4) Demonstrate the way in which decimal notation really involves an extension of the ordinary place value grid for whole numbers. In the same way that units (or ones) are ten times smaller than tens, tenths are ten times smaller than ones.

A dinosaur measuring 4.6m, recorded on a place value grid is:

HTU.$\frac{1}{10}$

4.6

(5) The familiar conventions for recording money as pounds and pence provide a useful way for introducing work with two decimal places.

Two whole pounds and thirty five pence = £2.35

One whole pound and five pence =   HTU.$\frac{1}{10}\frac{1}{100}$

£   1. 0 5

Fractional equivalences and calculations involving equivalences

Equivalent fractions can be introduced using a model of dividing/ splitting a whole into different numbers of pieces:

Where the lines divide the shapes you can see equivalences, for example $\frac{1}{4} = \frac{2}{8} = \frac{3}{12} = \frac{6}{24}$. Pupils understand halves and quarters as they meet

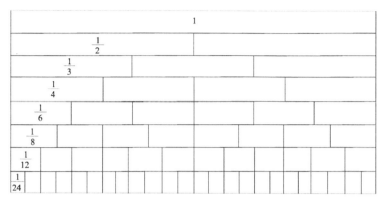

Figure 3.16 Equivalent fractions.

these fractions in everyday life and in ordinary language. When the fractions concept is related to simpler concepts for which pupils already have a visual image, dyslexic pupils are more likely to remember and understand them. By starting from this point a dyslexic pupil is more likely to understand the concept of $\frac{1}{2}$ of each of these items:

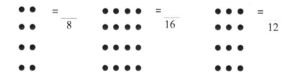

Figure 3.17a

or $\frac{1}{4}$ of each of these items:

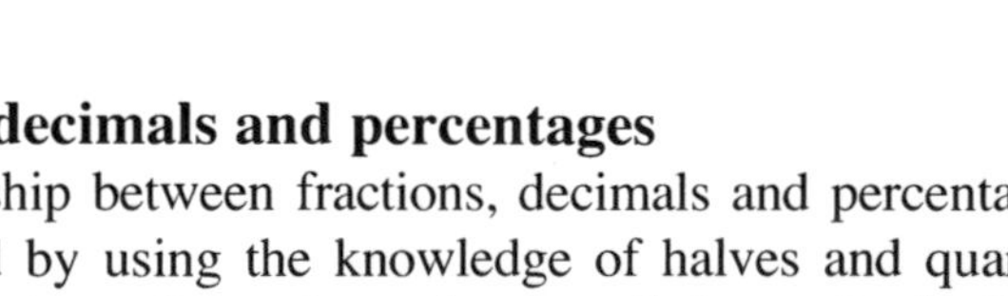

Figure 3.17b

Fractions, decimals and percentages

The relationship between fractions, decimals and percentages can be demonstrated by using the knowledge of halves and quarters which pupils already have. Secondary school pupils know that half is the same as 50% and £0.50 because these are everyday expressions. Using other facts they have learned, such as that $\frac{1}{4}$ is half of a half (shown by folding paper) and so half of 50% is 25%, this knowledge can be built upon.

One-quarter is 1 out of 4 parts so three-quarters is three lots of that, i.e. 75%.

Fraction	Decimal	Percentage
$\dfrac{1}{4}$	0.25	25%
$\dfrac{1}{2}$	0.5	50%
$\dfrac{3}{4}$	0.75	75%

Using the same digits makes it easy to see the link between decimals and the percentages.

The pupils' knowledge of money can be used to further these links. For example if you want $\frac{1}{10}$ of £1 it means cutting £1 into 10 parts, i.e. 10 × 10p pieces which is written £0.10. Per cent means out of one hundred so 10p, which is £$\frac{10}{100}$, is 10%. This leads to the further development of the conversion chart:

Fraction	Decimal	Percentage
$\dfrac{10}{100}$ or $\dfrac{1}{10}$	0.1	10%
$\dfrac{20}{100}$ or $\dfrac{2}{10}$ or $\dfrac{1}{5}$	0.2	20%
$\dfrac{70}{100}$ or $\dfrac{7}{10}$	0.7	70%
$\dfrac{89}{100}$	0.89	89%

Cards can be made containing equivalences between fractions, decimals and percentages. These cards can then be placed face down on the table and pupils can take turns to try to find the triples by turning over three cards at a time. This memory game will help to reinforce the equivalence of fractions, decimals and percentages.

Word problems

Simple real-life contexts can help to make some difficult concepts and calculations easier for pupils to understand. In this context, a number of word problem situations have already appeared in this book. Of course, curricula and examinations also require pupils to solve written word problems. Some dyslexic pupils are generally good problem solvers, but many dyslexic pupils find written word problems very difficult to solve.

Generally speaking, and reading problems aside, pupils who understand a word problem easily, recognise the type of problem that is in front of them. When a problem type is recognised, pupils are able to quickly select the operation required, locate the numbers embedded in the problem, and carry out the relevant calculation. This is called top-down problem solving. On the other hand, when pupils do not immediately know how to solve a given problem, this is because the problem type provides a conceptual challenge to the pupil. The first job of bottom-up problem solvers is to try to make sense of the situation, or problem type, which is contained within the word problem. Then the pupil has to try to figure out a solution, or match the situation to a calculation procedure he or she has learned.

The top-down/bottom-up distinction helps explain why some pupils solve certain problems very easily, but are poor at solving other problems. It is also important for teachers to understand that the successful bottom-up solution of a word problem helps to foster the pupil's understanding of the word problem type. On the other hand, when a pupil is unable to make sense of the word problem type, he or she will frequently adopt a tactic which tries to get the problem out of the way, but which does not involve any learning.

One tactic which failing bottom-up pupils frequently adopt, is the pragmatic one of looking at the size and nature of the numbers in order to select the most likely operation. For example, if a pupil has not yet learned how to complete long multiplication calculations, the pupil will be able to deduce that a problem containing the numbers 278 and 426 is not likely to involve a multiplication calculation.

Dyslexic pupils frequently need to be supported in becoming confident bottom-up problem solvers. Part of the problem for bottom-up problem solvers, and especially for any problem solver with language difficulties, is that word problems are expressed in extremely condensed and formulaic ways. In early written problem solving activities in each area of maths:

- The problem should be expressed in the simplest possible way. The language should be as natural and ordinary as possible.

Teachers should ensure that pupils understand all of the words that are used in the problems.

- Situations which pupils find genuinely engaging should be used whenever possible.
- Concrete materials may be made available to the pupil. Pupils should attempt to figure out a solution first, then check their solution, using the concrete materials.
- Simple, clear drawings could accompany some written word problems. For example, stick figures of people could accompany a sharing division problem. Alternatively pupils can be encouraged to draw pictures, or little diagrams to give themselves additional cognitive support.
- The working memory demands of early bottom-up problem solving mean that pupils should be permitted to simply record the solution to the word problem with some steps along the way, without necessarily thinking about and recording the formal operation which is involved. In the early stages of learning to write down problems, and record the steps of their solutions, pupils may be encouraged to use informal recording forms, such as the missing number format: $5 + \_ = 11$ or $5 \times \_ = 15$. This can be a helpful intermediate step when pupils are learning to solve division problems and comparison problems, or when they are using complementary addition to solve a subtraction problem.
- Consideration should be given to the reading ability of individual dyslexic pupils. Some pupils may require that word problems are read to them. Some benefit from structured practice at reading common word problem words, such as 'altogether'. Some pupils do well when special words which feature in the word problems, like the word chocolates, for example, are practised just ahead of the word problem session. The names of the people who feature in word problems, and the names of places, are often very hard to read. Dyslexic pupils can be encouraged to refer to difficult names by their initial letters, for example 'Sebastian' as 'S', Mr Thompson as Mr T.
- Pupils can be asked to make up word problems to fit specified situations, such as 'Make up a word problem which has a division with a remainder in it'; or specified calculations, such as 'Make up a word problem for the maths sentence, $4 \times 15 = ?$'. Making up word problems helps pupils understand how questions are constructed.

The word problem solving ability of dyslexic pupils can be further developed by:

- Making the language used in the word problems progressively difficult, condensed and word problem-like.
- Progressively targeting the more difficult word problem types which pupils are required to solve in given areas; for example, as well as solving ordinary 'equivalent groups' multiplication problems, dyslexic pupils should have practice at solving more difficult 'rate' multiplication problems such as '1 chocolate costs 8p. What will 5 chocolates cost?'; or the much harder: '2 packets of chocolates cost 50p. What will 10 packets of chocolates cost?'
- Making the structure or word order of word problems progressively difficult.
- Spending time on the study skills aspect of word problem solving. For example, teach the use of a problem solving frame:

  (a) Read the problem carefully.
  (b) Identify the key information.
  (c) Decide which calculation is necessary.
  (d) Select and use an appropriate calculation method: mental, written or using a calculator.
  (e) Check the answer in the context of the problem.

Shape, space and measures

It is often asked why educationalists concentrate on the numerical difficulties of dyslexics. The simple answer is that this is the area that causes dyslexic pupils the most significant problems. A four-year study of a sample of 82 dyslexic pupils of average and above intellectual ability found that over 50% of them failed to achieve Level 5 in Number Work, where Level 5 is appropriate for this age group. This compares with 27% in Measure, Space and Shape, and 18% in Handling Data who failed to achieve this target level. The relative success rate in the latter categories is partly due to the fact that much of the work in these areas is visual, and easily linked to real-life situations and is not purely abstract.

Even so there are areas within these categories that can cause particular difficulties for the dyslexic student:

Measures

Units of measurement

These cause difficulties for dyslexic learners because many of the words used to describe them have similar beginnings and endings, for example millimetre, millilitre, kilogram and kilometre. Pupils with reading difficulties can have significant problems distinguishing between these words. Abbreviations for the units of measurement (e.g. mm, ml, kg, km etc.) also have to be learnt, and how they relate to each other (e.g. 10 mm = 1 cm, or 1000 ml = 1l). All of these learning demands represent a significant memory pressure.

Converting between imperial and metric measurements is also particularly hard, as pupils tend to use certain measurements for particular things. For example they will measure cookery ingredients in grams but will usually weigh themselves in stones and pounds; they will measure the length of a book with their ruler in centimetres, but they may measure themselves in feet and inches!

A good deal of practical measuring needs to be done. This helps pupils become familiar with the measurements and to feel confident swapping between them. Pupils can be encouraged to remember a few measurements and work up or down in size from there. If pupils start with their own height and weight in both imperial and metric measurements, this is likely to be remembered because it involves personal information. Other measurements can then be compared with the targeted information.

In the initial stages of using a ruler, teachers should check that the pupil starts from the zero. Many dyslexic learners start measuring from 1.

In measuring work, pupils should be encouraged to estimate the measurements, first. This fosters a habit of thinking about how big something is likely to be in maths problems.

Scales

Using measurement scales can be difficult for dyslexic students, especially when they have to measure beyond the simple gradations increasing in ones. Numerical difficulties play a part here, because many pupils have difficulty remembering the sequences of numbers. However, most scales increase in 1s, 2s, 5s or 10s. This means that the work done with these patterns in the number part of the syllabus will be useful here. Using scales provides an ideal opportunity to revise these patterns and build on the work done with coins. Pupils will be able to see the link between different parts of maths. Because the elements of maths are interlinked, dyslexic learners begin to see that what they learn in one area can help them with another.

Area and perimeter

In area and perimeter work, it is usually the numerical elements, once again, that cause difficulty, rather than the measure concept *per se*. Dyslexic pupils often have difficulty with the multiple addition and multiplication aspects of solving perimeter and area problems.

Pupils should be encouraged to revise the bonds to ten so that they can execute the multiple additions in perimeter work efficiently. Once pupils have understood the concept that area is counted in squares they should be encouraged to use the most efficient way of calculating the total number of squares. This will involve revisiting multiplication strategies. For instance, four rows of six squares can be counted but it is more efficient to double six and double again. The calculation strategy is reinforced by the visual image of the rectangle.

As dyslexic pupils progress to more complicated area work, it is necessary to return to what they already know. For example when pupils are learning how to work out the area of the triangle it is more likely to stay in their memory if it can be linked to a fact that they have already learned. Allowing pupils to cut a rectangle in half, and placing one part on top of the other, helps them understand that the area of the triangle is half that of the rectangle.

With irregular shapes, perimeter work becomes more difficult; for instance, unknown sides may have to be calculated before the full perimeter can be added up. Pupils with spatial difficulties often have problems understanding the ways in which the sides of a shape relate to each other and have difficulty working out which numbers to use when finding the area of complex shapes. For example:

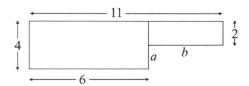

Figure 3.18 Finding unknown sides in perimeter.

To find the perimeter pupils need to see that $4 = 2 + a$, so $a = 2$, and $11 = b + 6$, so $b = 5$.

To find the area, pupils could use the 6 × 4 calculation for the first rectangle but they would need to figure out that $b = 5$ in order to calculate the other rectangle.

Both of these methods use algebra to find the missing number. They will need to be explained thoroughly as algebraic concepts can be too abstract for dyslexic pupils.

The best way of introducing these topics is via practical work. For example

(a) Pupils draw the shape on squared paper
(b) Pupils count to find the missing sides
(c) Pupils are shown how the solution can be calculated without drawing.

In this way, the algebra is anchored in real terms so that pupils can remember where it comes from and have a visual image to link it to.

Similarly, finding the surface area of a 3D shape can be difficult for pupils with spatial difficulties. This is because they are not able to visualise the part of the shape that they cannot see. Manipulating solid blocks is the best way of helping them to see what 'hidden faces' look like. It is also possible to cut out rectangles to cover a cuboid so that pupils can see how you arrive at the different sizes.

Time

Time is a topic that causes great difficulties for dyslexic students. There are so many different ways of saying the same thing; for example ten to seven can also be called 6:50 a.m. or p.m., or 06:50 or 18:50. Indeed time is often not written as we say it at all: nowhere in this list are the numbers 10 or 7! As we have seen, sequencing problems mean that many dyslexic learners cannot remember the correct order of the days of the week or of the months of the year. As the pupils progress to higher levels of mathematics they are asked to work out intervals of time. It is confusing for pupils to work in a base of 60 rather than in the more usual base of 10. Finally, reading of timetables can be particularly difficult for those students who have spatial or directional problems; they will not be able to track down one line and along another to find a certain time. To help dyslexic pupils:

(i) Days of the week and months of the year can be written on a set of cards and tied together in such a way that they cannot go out of sequence. The cards should be regularly revisited until the sequences are memorised.

(ii)   A good deal of time should be spent with a real clock face. 'On the hour' and 'half past the hour' should be understood first.

(iii) The early stages of understanding the terms 'past the hour' and 'to the hour' can be fostered in the following way. If an event starts at a selected time, on the hour, the pupil can be encouraged to calculate the amount of time that has gone *past* since the event started. For times which are on the 'to' side of the clock, the pupil considers the amount of time you have to wait until you get *to* the event.

(iv)   Watches or clocks which have different colours distinguishing one side of the clock from the other also help pupils to distinguish between past and to.

(v)   If pupils have learned to count in 5s during the number parts of the syllabus, this is a good time to revisit this skill. Counting in 5s around the clock leads towards an understanding of a digital representation of time. Digital time is generally easier for the pupils to learn as they have more experience of this in everyday life. For example the clocks on video recorders, cookers, televisions, and electric alarm clocks, all display digital time. Many pupils have digital watches. Finally, all timetables use this mode of writing time.

(vi)   For pupils with spatial difficulties, using of a right-angled piece of card to guide the eyes down one column and along another column makes reading from a timetable possible.

Shape and space

In shape and space work, there are many new mathematical words that dyslexic pupils have to learn. Words such as trapezium, isosceles, equilateral, parallelogram, symmetry etc. are all words that are specific to mathematics and are very difficult to remember and spell. Pupils will benefit from using rehearsal cards to learn new words. The cards should have the associated picture drawn on the reverse. When new words are introduced, teachers should link them with concepts already understood by the student. In *tri*angle, *tri* means three, as in three wheels on a *tri*cycle or three legs on a *tri*pod. In *quad*rilateral, *quad* means four as in four wheels on a *quad* bike. *Horizon*tal is straight across the page like the *horizon* where the sea meets the sky, etc.

Diagrams

Drawing shapes, both in 2D and 3D, drawing and measuring angles, symmetry and rotation work and coordinate work can cause difficulties for several reasons. Firstly, younger dyslexic pupils may not be able to retain an accurate picture of shapes or angles in their minds. Those with coordination problems may find it difficult to hold a ruler in one hand while using the pencil with the other. Coordination becomes even more difficult when pupils progress onto using a compass to draw circles, or protractors to draw and measure angles, as the techniques may prove difficult. Drawing a 3D shape can be even more difficult as pupils are expected to draw what they see and they may not be able to focus on the distinguishing parts of the shape. Further difficulties with spatial imaging may occur when a student is asked to draw a 2D representation of a 3D shape. Similarly it can be difficult for a dyslexic pupil to imagine the way a shape will look on the other side of a mirror line. This is particularly true if the line of symmetry is on a diagonal. It is equally difficult for some dyslexics to visualise shapes after they have been turned through a number of degrees and they will have to learn the significance of 90°, 180°, 270° and 360°. Directional confusion can make fixing points on a grid problematic. Dyslexic pupils can be helped in the following ways:

(i) In the early stages, students should manipulate plastic shapes in order to build a kinaesthetic memory of the shapes. Pupils should be encouraged to draw around the shape, or learn to put a dot at each corner so they can join up the dots to construct the shape.

(ii) The use of isometric paper helps some pupils to draw in 3D. Even with this aid, some students who have spatial or coordination problems are unable to do this work easily. As well as having the solid shapes as visual aids, using unifix cubes to build up the shape in 3D can also make drawing easier.

(iii) Practice at using a ruler should be encouraged; drawing patterns with straight lines and joining up dots will improve pupils' control of rulers.

(iv) When using a pair of compasses for the first time, some pupils find it easier to keep the compasses still and move the page around.

(v) Initially emphasis must be put on following round from the zero on the protractor so that the pupil knows whether to look at the inside or outside line when measuring angles. Clockwise and anti-clockwise can be reinforced with the use of a clock.

(vi) Estimating as to whether an angle is bigger or smaller than 90° or 180° is essential so that a pupil is able to successfully self-check when reading the numbers off the protractor.

(vii) Mirrors and tracing paper are allowed in all examinations. In symmetry work, teachers should help pupils to use these tools to good effect.

(viii) A simple mnemonic such as 'along the corridor and up the stairs' may help with coordinates, along with the use of the right-angled card to help pupils to place points.

Handling data

Probability

Probability generally ties in with knowledge that pupils already have. A half and half or fifty-fifty chance of something happening is a phrase that is familiar to them. Pupils understand that if something is nearly impossible it is a very small chance and will be close to zero. Naming a probability as a fraction is generally understood. However the point at which probability becomes difficult for a dyslexic student is when they have to deal with fractions! Fraction work was covered earlier in this chapter.

Averages

Averages tend to cause problems for dyslexic students because the vocabulary is difficult. Mean, median and mode are all averages but it is confusing that pupils have to perform different calculations for each type.

Repetition and mnemonics help, for example *mo*de is the *mo*st frequent, me*di*an is the mi*ddl*e value and me*an* is the *a*verage. Cards which include these explanations can be introduced into the student's personal learning pack to try to commit these terms to memory. The multiple additions which are part of averages work represent a good opportunity to rehearse addition strategies.

Graphs

Graphs can be problematic for pupils with spatial awareness difficulties. Number difficulties affect the ability of pupils to understand the scales on the axes of graphs. Dyslexic pupils can find pie charts confusing because they have to use a protractor rather than a ruler. Number difficulties also affect the ability of pupils to work with percentages in pie chart work.

When pupils draw graphs, initially the axes can be drawn for them. This helps pupils to fix the image of the graph forms in their minds. Practice with rulers is involved when pupils draw blocks. The scales on a graph tend to be structured in 1s, 2s, 5s, or 10s and so reinforcement of the patterns of these numbers can occur here. Drawing and measuring with pie chart scales tends to come with practice. Finding percentages of given amounts has been described in a previous section.

Chapter 4

Further Help for Dyslexic Learners and Concluding Remarks

Some planning and management suggestions

In order to prepare for teaching dyslexic students there are several levels of intervention and management that staff can employ.

The first is simply to raise awareness, among the whole school staff in primary schools, or the mathematics department in secondary schools, of the difficulties faced by these students when learning mathematics, as discussed in previous chapters of this book. This applies not only to the qualified teaching staff but also to the classroom assistants who may be dealing with these pupils in a support role.

Secondly an agreement should be reached on the overall structure of the syllabus. For example a spiral structure where topics are regularly revisited and built upon is advocated in the NNS and it is essential to continue this in secondary school. Not only does a spiral programme help to overcome memory weaknesses, by regularly revising topics, but it also allows pupils to have access to a variety of mathematical areas so that they can succeed in at least one of them. This helps to improve the pupil's self-esteem.

A whole school policy should be entered into on many aspects of teaching mathematics to dyslexic students. For example, primary school teachers will need to have a coherent policy on how the maths facts, such as the times tables facts, are to be learnt, and rehearsed by dyslexic pupils. It is also useful to have a clearly understood policy on homework. The choice of textbooks and examination material is crucial. All written materials must be accessible to dyslexic students and therefore the language element of materials should be as brief or limited as possible.

An agreement should be reached on the types of concrete materials or cognitive tools to be used by teachers to help support written resources, and on which types will be made available for dyslexic pupils in all classes. This will ensure that there is continuity for the pupils throughout the school, that pupils become familiar with the tools as early in their maths learning careers as possible and that they are not embarrassed to use them. It is important to ensure that individual students understand the materials which teachers use with them. Materials should lend themselves to progressively developing uses, to cater for the fact that students have to deal with increasingly complicated maths content.

Teachers must agree upon the calculation methods that work best with individual pupils and liaison will need to take place between teachers and support staff if the pupil is not to become confused by too many different methods. This liaison must also take place between primary and secondary schools. For example, state primary schools generally follow the guidelines established in the Numeracy Strategy, which state that the teaching of standard algorithms should be delayed until the end of Year 3, or until the pupil is ready to learn them. In practice, this means that a dyslexic pupil may not be introduced to the standard methods until Year 5 or 6 and the pupil will probably not have had much time to practise the standard methods. If secondary school teachers expect that all pupils will be competent at using standard methods this can lead to difficulties.

There is a lot of evidence to show that the learning style of a dyslexic pupil may have an effect on his or her ability to successfully learn mathematics. A teacher who insists on a particular style of processing problems, or who insists on the use of particular calculation methods, risks alienating pupils who think and learn in a different way. Following Chinn and Ashcroft (1998), we have already described the different cognitive style extremes as the inchworm and grasshopper styles respectively.

To test for learning at a younger age, it is possible to set a few appropriate tasks and interview the child once a solution is reached, asking the simple question, 'How did you do that?' In this way, teachers will be able to identify which strategies are being employed, how mature or inventive the child's strategies are, and whether the strategies are successfully used. In very general terms, excessive use of mechanical counting solutions frequently indicates that a younger dyslexic pupil is an inchworm in orientation.

The Thinking Style Test (Chinn, 2002) can be used with secondary or older primary school pupils, as a means of identifying the type of strategies that an individual uses when trying to solve mathematical problems. The test requires pupils to answer mathematical questions such as, 'There are 25 squares in the diagram below, how many have a cross?'

X	X	X	X	X
X				X
				X
X				X
X	X	X	X	X

An inchworm would count the squares around the edge or might count in fives, showing a step-by-step approach. A grasshopper would see that there was a block of 9 in the middle and one more empty square to make 10. There are 25 altogether so 25 − 10 is 15, showing a more holistic approach to solving the problem.

Although it would seem that dyslexic pupils, in general, tend to use a procedure-orientated style more often than their non-dyslexic counterparts, it is often helpful for teachers to identify those dyslexic pupils who are grasshopper in orientation. This is because it is possible to enhance the adolescent dyslexic grasshopper's natural style by introducing him or her to different methods or strategies for solving a problem. We have noted that some dyslexic pupils are able to devise alternative strategies for themselves, but most dyslexic students will need to be taught useful non-standard calculation methods in order to overcome the kinds of difficulties they have with learning mathematics. Grasshoppers are also able to make better progress when they are prepared for a possible failure of a scheme or solution process, and are encouraged to have another one in reserve, particularly in order to check their calculations.

Before designing specific programmes of work, teachers should be prepared to assess their pupils using a diagnostic approach to maths testing. Analysing pupils' responses to questions in a diagnostic way allows teachers to find out where the strengths, weaknesses and gaps of the pupils lie. It also enables teachers to aim work at an appropriate level. An appropriate teaching level should always start from the point where a student feels comfortable so that teachers can build on a sound knowledge base. For diagnostic purposes, teachers may choose to devise their own tests; they may use some of the many different kinds of test booklets which are commercially available; alternatively, they may choose to use a standardised maths test.

Some standardised tests which can be used for diagnostic purposes include:

(1) Wide Range Achievement Test (WRAT3), Dyslexia Institute. This test covers ages from 6 to 75 years and takes 15 minutes. It is a numeracy test with no word problems.

(2) Basic Number Screening Test, Hodder and Stoughton. This tests pupils from 7 to 12 years and again deals with numeracy. It takes 30 minutes to complete and can be read to the pupils.

(3) Graded Arithmetic Mathematics Test, Hodder and Stoughton. This tests pupils from 5 to 12 years and takes about 30 minutes to complete. It mainly tests number but does have a few questions on measure and handling data and contains a diagnosis for all areas.

(4) Mathematics Competency Test, Hodder and Stoughton. This tests pupils from 11 to 17 years and takes 30 minutes to administer. It is again mainly number but has some work on time, graphs etc.

All the standardised tests mentioned above give an approximate mathematics age for a pupil so that it is possible to see how far behind in maths learning terms the pupils are. However, much more information can be gleaned if the errors of the pupil are carefully analysed. To find out as much as possible about how individual pupils do maths, teachers may choose to administer tests in an informal way, asking pupils question such as 'How did you work it out?' as the test proceeds.

The role of consultation

The number of experts in the field of mathematics and dyslexia is few and therefore the role of consultation tends to be more limited than it is with literacy difficulties. However, some useful information can be gleaned from an educational psychologist's report. For example:

- The scores that dyslexic students achieve on the arithmetic element of the WISC test are generally poor. This is because the test is done as mental arithmetic and relies largely on the short-term memory of the student. This means that if the score is above 10 (average) you may well have a potentially good mathematician on your hands.
- The digit span element is worth looking at as it gives an indication of the amount of material a student can deal with at any one time. For example students with a digit span of three cannot recall numbers with more than three digits from their memory. Therefore trying to do any questions that involve thousands, hundreds, tens and units with that student will be very difficult.

The standardised test results give a little more information on the ability of the pupil. However the information is no substitute for carrying out your own assessment where you can see the paper, analyse the mistakes and ask the pupil to describe how they performed a calculation. Please see the resources section later in this chapter for names of people and organisations who can be consulted.

Help with tests and examinations

Initially teachers will need to find out which areas of mathematics are the weakest for an individual student. Tests need to be performed and analysed in the topic areas so that weaknesses can be identified. It is necessary to encourage students to use calculation methods that suit them best. Teachers should note down the methods pupils use effectively. If students are consistently encouraged to verbalise their methods it is more likely that these will be committed to long-term memory. Teachers should be prepared to take students back to a level at which they can achieve success. This can be done by using easier examples or by revisiting an earlier stage in the development of that concept, before gradually building on the firm foundation achieved.

Preparation for examinations relies heavily on building familiarity with the type of questions that are likely to be asked. Many dyslexic pupils see new maths questions as completely different problems from ones they have met before, even those based on the same topic. It is therefore necessary to expose the pupil to many versions of the same type of question to ensure that confusion does not follow in an examination as a result of a different format or wording. For example, many pupils would be able to answer the question: $4 + 7 =$ ___ , but would have difficulty with $4 +$ ___ $= 11$ if they had not previously seen this format or had time to verbalise the question. Teachers need to ensure that pupils have learned the age-appropriate specialised maths vocabulary and language, for example 'Give the product of 16 and 8'. Pupils should be encouraged to look for links in the topics they are studying. They should be reminded that they will be able to use the facts they have committed to long-term memory to enable them to reach new or difficult answers. For example, a pupil may know that 2×5 is ten because they have committed their doubles to memory. They should then be encouraged to see that 4×5 is double the double, using already known facts. Preparation for the National Curriculum Key Stage tests or Common Entrance tests will take the form of revision and practice to ensure that familiarity. There are many practice books and papers available so that pupils can read through and become familiar with the types of questions that they will be asked in the actual examinations. Additional revision questions can be devised which target those topics or question types that pupils find particularly difficult.

Examination skills and techniques will need to be taught to most dyslexic students and practice under test conditions will be helpful. Advice given to individuals will vary according to their particular personalities and areas of difficulty. There are some students who rush through a paper just to get it finished and make careless mistakes along the way. Such pupils will obviously need to be encouraged to slow down or to go back and check their work when they have finished the paper. Other students cannot remember how to complete a particular question and tend to waste a large amount of time trying to do so. These students should be encouraged to leave that question and go on to another which they can do, returning to the difficult one at the end, if time allows. However it should be stressed that individual analysis of examination technique is essential in order for appropriate guidance to be given to specific pupils. For example, a particular student who was taught by one of the authors did not ever finish a paper and left many gaps along the way. It was possible to think, therefore, that he had a very low level in mathematics, had a very weak memory and worked very slowly. On questioning him, however, and watching him perform, it was evident that he had both the memory and ability to attempt the questions. In fact, he was 90% of his way through a question when he decided he had spent too long on that answer and moved on without writing any of it down. Guidance was given in terms of writing steps down as he went through the paper so that he could pick up working marks, and organising his time better so that he could go back and finish some of the questions when he reached the end.

By the time pupils are 16, they will be required to undertake a public examination and the selection of an appropriate GCSE syllabus is clearly important. Different examining groups produce different types of examination paper. A dyslexic pupil can be helped to show his true potential if he is entered into the most appropriate examination.

The following general criteria should be employed when choosing a suitable examination paper or textbooks for dyslexic students:

* Dyslexic pupils need help to retrieve information from their memory and a multi-sensory teaching approach is the best aid here. When teaching a dyslexic child it is important to alternate between careful but succinct exposition, demonstration, practical work, discussions and abstract over-learning practice (Chinn and Ashcroft, 1998). When work is presented orally and visually and practical work is designed to give a motor and tactile input, the student is able to file away the new topic multi-sensorally and is generally able to retrieve it more easily. Wherever possible, examination papers and books should use pictorial representations and/or diagrams. This frequently helps a dyslexic student to retrieve the information by calling upon both auditory and visual senses.
* Mental arithmetic sections of examinations are timed and rely on good working-memory resources. This form of test tends to be very difficult for dyslexic pupils and so a course without a separate mental arithmetic paper should be sought, if possible.

- Papers should be chosen which allow students to adopt a range of different solution approaches. They should allow for points to be given for correct partial steps or workings (to suit inchworms) as well as awarding full marks for a correct answer, without requiring that workings are shown (to suit grasshoppers). Textbooks for older students should provide explanations of different methods to allow pupils to choose their preferred mode of working.
- It is important to choose papers and textbooks that use simple language. Questions should be well-spaced, as uncluttered as possible, and should use the minimum number of words. This allows dyslexic pupils to focus on what is required of them mathematically without becoming anxious about the literacy element.
- As we have seen, most dyslexic pupils have problems with sequencing. A complicated problem, which may, for example, require three calculations in sequence, might overload the working memory of a dyslexic pupil. Papers and books should be chosen which present complex questions in several individual steps.
- Spatial awareness can also be a problem for some dyslexic pupils. It is helpful to look for papers and books that have grids in place. Axes should be drawn so that graphs can be successfully attempted.
- Papers and textbooks should not require dyslexic pupils to write pages of explanation when a few words and symbols would suffice.

No examining group has designed papers specifically for dyslexic pupils. No complete set of textbooks has been written to cater for the complex needs of dyslexic pupils, either. This means that it is unlikely that staff will find materials that will fulfil all criteria. However there are some materials and examination papers which are more appropriate for dyslexic pupils than others. This is because many non-dyslexic pupils also benefit from papers and books which use simple language, are well-spaced, and have clear diagrams etc.

The SMP Graduated Assessment GCSE examined by OCR fulfils many of the above criteria. This course has the additional benefit of being modular so that a pupil can concentrate on a given number of topics, do a test on them and then move on to a different group of topics. Therefore dyslexic students do not have to hold all the topics in their minds in one go until the final paper. By that stage they have already taken 50% of the marks towards their GCSE.

Specific types of help available

Many factors make succeeding in examinations very difficult for dyslexic pupils. However, the following allowances can be made in the National Curriculum end of Key Stage tests in mathematics.

It is readily accepted that dyslexic pupils will take longer to reach the result of a calculation. This is due to long-term memory deficits, which means that pupils have to use alternative strategies to answer the questions. Therefore in the National Curriculum end of Key Stage tests pupils are allowed an extra 25% of time if they have a Statement of Educational Needs or are at the 'School Action' or 'School Action Plus' of the SEN Code of Practice. However no extra time is given in the mental arithmetic section. Dyslexic pupils have to undertake the taped versions of this test with all other pupils. It has been decided that the few additional seconds that would be granted with 25% extra time are 'unlikely to be helpful'.

Pupils who have difficulty concentrating for long periods of time are allowed rest breaks at natural breaking points in the examinations. The clock is stopped for a few minutes to allow a pupil to refocus. The pupil must not discuss the paper during the break and must not exceed the given time limit of the examination. Pupils may also have a prompter who is able to draw their attention back to task by, for example, a light tap on the table.

If a pupil has difficulty reading a paper in mathematics, the teacher may read the questions to them. This concession will only be allowed if there is a significant disparity between the pupil's reading and chronological age, i.e. below 9 years for Key Stage 3 and below 10 years for Key Stage 4.

For some pupils the written elements of the papers will prove difficult. Their spelling may still be very weak, their speed of writing extremely slow or unintelligible under pressure. These pupils may use a transcription or an amanuensis to write the answers down for them. The schools must show that using an amanuensis is normal practice for the pupil if they are to use this facility.

In order to help with the visualisation of a question teachers can provide pupils with real objects, like those in the texts. For questions involving symmetry pupils may be given mirrors and tracing paper.

It should be noted that, despite the concessions mentioned above, a small minority of students will still find the examination process too stressful and may need to be exempted from these types of tests.

The mental arithmetic element in particular may prove too much for many dyslexic students due to the limited amount of time allowed for each calculation. However we would not recommend disapplication from the Key Stage tests just because of the mental arithmetic element.

Case studies of successes

1. *James*

James was 14 years old and was due to be sitting his Key Stage 3 test at the end of Year 9 with the rest of his peers. He was diagnosed dyslexic and his IQ score showed that he was of average ability. His maths age showed a deficit of five years and the Vernon/ Miller Graded Arithmetic Test showed weaknesses in multiple addition, multiplication, division, algebra (finding missing numbers), and fractions. His practice Key Stage 3 tests indicated an overall Level 4 with a relative strength in space and shape work but a big weakness in number (below Level 3), to the extent where he showed no strategies for basic computation and resorted to tallying as his only means of working. His self-esteem was very low and he would try to hide his inadequacy by quickly saying that he understood a new topic when he had not taken in anything, just so the teacher would not highlight him by standing there any longer.

This pupil needed individual support outside the classroom in order to allow him to admit his lack of knowledge and make progress by using concrete materials that he would not dream of allowing his peers to see him using in class.

The programme ran over a period of 12 weeks and consisted of one half-hour session a week with follow up exercises to do in private.

His targets were:

* to increase his maths age and NC level by taking him back to a level where he could achieve success and then building gently;
* to develop strategies for calculations, using visual memory when introducing a topic, reinforcing in space and shape work where possible;
* to improve self-esteem and belief by praise and careful targets.

The strategies used were:

(a) His number bonds to 10, 20 and 100 were practised to speed up addition and subtraction problems. These were reinforced in angle work and multiple addition calculations for averages.

Money was used as a concrete material and thus extended his knowledge into decimals.

(b) Alternative strategies for multiplication and division were reviewed again using coins and the doubling technique. This led to fraction work with halving.

(c) Missing numbers work was encouraged throughout to improve algebra and verbalising his methods was encouraged to reinforce the learning.

Methods described in the previous chapters were used in order to cover these areas with James. He was able to take on and use strategies for addition and multiplication which helped him with his speed of working and his understanding of algebra, fractions, decimals and percentages. His confidence in his own abilities increased greatly and his results in the final Key Stage 3 test indicated that he had improved his number to Level 4 from below a Level 3.

2. *Edward*

Edward was 9 years old. He was performing very poorly in maths at school and he often said he hated maths. Although his parents had practised the tables sequences intensively, he knew very few times tables by heart. He counted to work out many maths facts and sometimes used his fingers. An educational psychologist assessed him. He was found to have an above average ability but his individual scores indicated that he was dyslexic. His arithmetic score in the WISC (Wechsler Intelligence Scale for Children) was 9 and his digit span score was also 9. In the WOND Mathematics Reasoning Test he achieved a maths age of 7 years 4 months.

Edward received 1½ hours of maths tuition, with two other pupils, each week. His mother agreed to supervise working through Edward's rehearsal cards every day. All aspects of his tuition that he found difficult to remember were to be put onto the cards. It was stressed that his mother should show no signs of frustration if Edward had forgotten anything. It was also agreed that the main focus of Edward's tuition would be the times tables facts, but that other weak areas would be covered alongside tables work.

In the teaching programme, Edward:

(a) engaged in all aspects of the groups work described in Chapter 3

(b) was given a pack of four sets of *Number Pattern* cards; he played simple games with the cards at home; he was shown that he could use the number patterns to visualise missing number and subtraction questions; he continued to play games with the cards during the first term

(c) mastered the facts of ten, and subtraction from ten; Edward was able to generalise *Number Pattern* work and *Facts of ten* work to knowledge of the facts of all the counting numbers

(d) learned to halve tens numbers, such as 30 and 50

(e) started structured times tables sequence learning by working on the 5 × tables

(f) was shown how to bridge through ten to work calculations such as $8 + 5$, $14 - 6$, $24 - 6$

(g) extended his *Facts of ten* knowledge to subtractions from decade numbers such as $60 - 6$

(h) chose to learn the 4 × table sequence; in the following session, the 4 × and 5 × table sequences were mixed

(i) worked systematically through the tables sequences; more and more tables sequences were mixed

(j) built on his tables knowledge in a number of ways; he learned progressively difficult language: multiply, divide, product, multiple, factor, prime number; he learned to figure out short multiplication and short division questions

(k) completed work on the basic fractional forms

(l) solved sharing division problems; he then practised finding fractions of numbers, for example $\frac{2}{3}$ of 24.

Edward's confidence began to improve almost immediately and he announced that he liked maths. After one term he was moved to a higher set in maths at school. After two terms, it was agreed that he no longer needed intensive tuition, although Edward's mother agreed to continue with the rehearsal card idea for some time. It was also agreed that he would be given a further tuition top-up if he began to lose confidence again.

An outline of additional resources for further staff development

The main experts in the field of mathematics and dyslexia who can be contacted for advice, support or assessment are:

Dorian Yeo at Emerson House, London. (Primary School age)
Steve Chinn and Julie Kay at Mark College, Somerset.
Anne Henderson at St Davids College, Llandudno
Olwen El-Naggar at the National Association for Special
    Educational Needs
The Bangor Dyslexia Unit, University of Wales.
The Dyslexia Teaching Centre, Kensington Square, London.
Mahesh Sharma at Cambridge College, Massachusetts or through
    Patricia Brazil at Berkshire Mathematics.

The bibliography at the end of this book contains many excellent books that have been written on maths and dyslexia. However if further details of the ideas contained in this book are required, then we would recommend that you refer to:

Yeo, D. (2003) *Dyslexia, Dyspraxia and Mathematics*. London:
    Whurr Publishers.
Chinn, S. J. and Ashcroft, J. R. (1998) *Mathematics for Dyslexics*:
    A teaching handbook. 2nd edition. London: Whurr.
Miles, T. R. and E. (eds) (1992) *Dyslexia and Mathematics*. London:
    Routledge (second edition pending).

Articles on the latest developments in this area are often found in:

Dyslexia Handbook, *Dyslexia Contact* magazine and *Dyslexia Journal*, available through the BDA at 98 London Road, Reading.
Tel: 0118 966 8271
Dyslexia Review, available through the Dyslexia Institute.
Tel: 01784 463 851

Courses are run by:
(1) Steve Chinn and Julie Kay at Mark College. Tel: 01278 641632.
     E-mail: post@markcollege.somerset.sch.uk
(2) Dorian Yeo at Emerson House, London.
     E-mail: dyeo@blue yonder.co.uk. or www.dyeo.co.uk.
(3) Dyslexia Institute. Tel: 01784 463 851.
     E-mail: info@dyslexia-inst.org.uk
(4) Mahesh Sharma through Berkshire Mathematics. Tel: 0118 948
     3476. E-mail: trish@chazey.freeserve.co.uk

Concluding comments

We emphasise that all dyslexic pupils are individuals. As Chinn (2003) says, 'No two dyslexic individuals are the same. They show individual variations in abilities, attitudes and difficulties and thus differ in their special educational needs.' The previous learning experiences of dyslexic pupils also shape who they are. From a teaching point of view, the challenge is to find the most appropriate ways of helping the individual dyslexic pupil learn. The ideas and teaching suggestions that we describe in this book are ones which the authors have found have helped the majority of dyslexic pupils make progress. However, in teaching all aspects of maths, there are a number of different possible ways to proceed. In teaching pupils with such complex patterns of needs, it is important not to teach in set ways. Within the framework of the general teaching principles that we have outlined, and depending on the context in which the pupil is being taught, teachers might have to adapt methods or even invent new ones. While many pupils will benefit from most of the suggestions that we have made, teachers sometimes have to accept that a particular idea, method or material simply does not suit a particular pupil. They might have to try out a few different teaching ideas before they find ones which work.

Again, because pupils are individuals, they will make progress at different rates. At one end of the continuum of possible progress, some dyslexic pupils are able to make extremely rapid advances in maths when they are taught in a structured, understanding-based and multi-sensory way and are given sufficient memory support. On the other end of the continuum, some pupils need time to make progress. Many dyslexic pupils have periods when they make good progress, and other periods when they plateau and may even return to less-advanced ways of doing things. As we have emphasised, it is typical of most dyslexic pupils that they will forget aspects of maths they had learnt.

It is very important that teachers keep in mind the kinds of cognitive difficulties that affect the dyslexic pupil's ability to learn. The attitudes of teachers have a very profound influence on the overall learning outcome of any programme of teaching. If teachers remain positive and supportive, pupils will retain a positive self-belief. They will be helped to believe that they can and will make progress. On the other hand, impatience and a culture of blame promote a negative self-image and frequently make pupils anxious.

As we have noted, teachers should always be prepared to help put back what the dyslexic pupil may have forgotten. When teachers do this in a natural, accepting and blame-free way, dyslexic pupils will be able to view learning maths in a largely positive way. They will be helped to manage their maths difficulties effectively.

References

Chinn, S. J. (1995) 'A pilot study to compare aspects of arithmetic skills', *Dyslexia Review*, **7**(1), 4–7.

Chinn, S. J. (2002) *The Thinking Style Test*, Somerset: Mark College.

Chinn, S. J. (2003) 'CreSTed (Council for the Registration of Schools Teaching Dyslexics)', in *The Dyslexia Handbook*, 2003.

Chinn, S. J. and Ashcroft, J. R. (1998) *Mathematics for Dyslexics: A teaching handbook*. 2nd edition. London: Whurr.

Chinn, S., McDonagh, D., van Elswijk, R., Harmsen, H., Kay, J., McPhillips, T., Power, A. and Skidmore, L. (2001) 'Classroom studies into cognitive style in mathematics for pupils with dyslexia in special education in the Netherlands, Ireland and the U.K.', in *British Journal of Special Education*, Vol. 28, No. 2 pp. 80–85.

Miles, T. R. and Miles, E. (eds) (1992) *Dyslexia and Mathematics*, London: Routledge.

Thompson, I. (ed.) (1999) *Issues in teaching numeracy in primary schools*, London: OUP.

Yeo, D. (2003) *Dyslexia, Dyspraxia and Mathematics*, London: Whurr.

Additional Bibliography

Ashcraft, M. H., Kirk, E. P. and Hopko, D. (1988) 'On the cognitive consequences of mathematics anxiety', in C. Donlan (ed.) *The Development of Mathematical Skills*, Hove, East Sussex: Psychology Press.

Butterworth, B. (1999) *The Mathematical Brain*, London: Macmillan.

Chinn, S. J. (2000) 'Dyslexic pupils learning in the Numeracy Strategy', in *The Dyslexia Handbook*, 2000.

Chinn, S. J. (2000) *What to do when you can't learn the times tables*, Baldock: Egon.

Chinn, S. J., Kay, J. and Skidmore, L. (2001) *Worksheets Plus for the Numeracy Strategy, Years 4 and 5*, Baldock: Egon.

Dehaene, S. (1997) *The Number Sense*, London: Penguin Books.

Dehaene, S., Spelke, E., Pinet, R. and Tsivkin, S. (1999) 'Sources of mathematical thinking: behavioural and brain-imaging evidence', in *Science*, Vol. 284, pp. 970–973.

El Naggar, O. (1996) *Specific Learning Difficulties in Mathematics: A classroom approach*, Tamworth: NASEN.

Gray, E. (1997) 'Compressing the counting process: developing a flexible interpretation of symbols', in I. Thompson (ed.) *Teaching and learning early number*, Buckingham: OUP.

Grauberg, E. (1998) *Elementary Mathematics and Language Difficulties*, London: Whurr.

Henderson, A. (2000) *Maths for the Dyslexic: A practical guide*, London: David Fulton.

Hiebert, J., Carpenter, T., Fennema, E., Fuson, K., Wearne, D., Murray, H., Olivier, A. and Human, P. (1997) *Making Sense: Teaching and learning maths with understanding*, Portsmouth: Heinemann.

Palti, G. (2003) 'Dyslexia and Resilience', in *The Dyslexia Handbook*, 2003.

Sharma, M. C. (1986) 'Dyscalculia and other learning problems in arithmetic: a historical perspective', in *Focus on Learning Problems in Mathematics*, **8**, (3,4).

Thompson, I. (ed.) (1997) *Teaching and learning early number*, London: OUP.

Wright, R. J., Martland, J., Stafford, A. K. and Stanger, G. (2002) *Teaching Number: Advancing children's skills and strategies*, London: Paul Chapman.

Yeo, D. (2002) 'Newer Approaches to Teaching Maths to Primary Children', in *The Dyslexia Handbook*, 2002.

Yeo, D. (2003) 'A Brief Overview of Some Contemporary Methodologies in Primary Maths', in *The Dyslexia Handbook*, 2003.

Note: The Dyslexia Handbooks are published annually by The British Dyslexia Association: The Handbook 2000 is edited by I. Smythe, 2002 and 2003 by M. Johnson and L. Peer.

Index